Dream Power

Can Our Dreams Make Us Well?

Mary Jo Davis-Grant

SterlingHouse Publisher, Inc.   Pittsburgh, PA

Dream Power

DREAM POWER:
Can Our Dreams Make Us Well?
MARY JO DAVIS-GRANT
crone@southwind.net

Best Book in Psychology - 2007

ISBN 1-58501-095-2
Trade Paperback
© Copyright 2007 Mary Jo Davis-Grant
All Rights Reserved
Library of Congress #2006922167

Requests for information should be addressed to:
SterlingHouse Publisher, Inc.
7436 Washington Avenue
Pittsburgh, PA 15218
info@sterlinghousepublisher.com
www.sterlinghousepublisher.com

SterlingHouse Books
is an imprint of SterlingHouse Publisher, Inc.

SterlingHouse Publisher, Inc.
is a company of CyntoMedia Corporation.

Cover Design: Jamie Linder
Original Artwork By: Jamie Linder
Interior Design: Kathleen M. Gall

Printed in U.S.A.

DEDICATION

In Underhill (1961) Mechtilde of Magdeberg is quoted, "The writing of this book was seen, heard and experienced in every limb. I see it with the eyes of my soul and hear it with the ears of my eternal spirit" (p. 84).

I can only say AMEN. I feel exposed, vulnerable and strangely clear, almost transparent and very, very grateful that I have been gifted with this experience.

I dedicate this work to my family for loving and praying me through this project. To my husband I am especially grateful. He knows well how many frustrating hours I spent trying to deal objectively with such a mass of subjective material. His quiet confidence never wavered. My daughter and my son kept me focused by repeating, "Mom, just tell your story." To my grandsons, I leave my story as a testament that age should never be an obstacle to growth and change.

TABLE OF CONTENTS

ABSTRACT

During the late 1980's, I suffered from chronic physical pain. Over a seven-year period, using Biogenics, I experienced an extraordinary holistic recovery mediated by spontaneous waking dreams that were filled with archetypal images. This study addresses this specific research question: Is it possible to track the interaction of the archetypal images on my body's chakra energy system accessed through Biogenics with the holistic healing I experienced? This research process is an analysis of 41 of the 500 waking dreams that I recorded over the seven years of healing (2,500 days). These dreams were selected for the degree of personal impact they had on me, and how representative they were of the recurring themes and archetypal images. They were selected before the following analytical procedure was constructed. The date of the waking dream is given so its chronology and progression is clear; second, the waking dream is described; third, I discuss the archetypal image and its effect on me (physically, psychologically, and/or spiritually) and the issues in my life it addresses; fourth, I identify and discuss the chakras affected. A summary of each waking dream is provided. The results of this analysis suggest that the healing process progressed through physical, psychological, and spiritual issues, and that each level of healing occurred while I was experiencing a progression of waking dreams. These dreams moved from predominately tribal archetypal images to spiritual archetypal images. The chakras affected tended to move from activity in the lower chakras to the upper chakras. A strong case suggests that the answer to the research question is *Yes*, the healing I experienced can be traced to the interaction of archetypal images with my chakra energy system. Three major implications of the study are: (1) healing can be accessed through imagery: (2) archetypal healing could become a significant partner with many other healing modalities for many dis-eases: and (3) Biogenics, which provides a safe, drug-free method of pain and stress management, can serve as the catalyst for archetypal healing. Recommendations for further study are given.

ACKNOWLEDGEMENTS

So many good people were critical to the completion of this writing project. Norm Shealy and his staff at the Shealy Pain Clinic were the catalysts who started me on my healing journey. Lou Piech helped me to identify strengths that I was unaware of and thereby gave me a great gift. Len Evans introduced me to the world of dreams and images. Caroline Myss and Norm Shealy provided a conceptual framework for my healing experiences. My dissertation committee consisting of Bob Nunley, Norm Shealy, and Berney Williams were thoughtful and kind whenever I had problems and their consideration during my oral examination was much appreciated. Sandy Seward was so gracious with her time and expertise and provided essential personal support, advice, and insight. Arlys-Marie Gilchrist and her technical computer skills were invaluable to the successful completion of this product.

Looking back, it seems that this experience has been essentially a prayer experience from beginning to end. I acknowledge those many prayer partners who have lifted me and sustained me by their prayers. I have truly been gifted with grace. It is my prayer that my story will be a gift to you.

LIST OF FIGURES

LIST OF TABLES

PREFACE

Throughout the preparation of this dissertation, the concern has been that the nature and themes of this work may be too subjective for consideration by traditional academic standards. It was a relief to be referred by my dissertation committee to *Transpersonal Research Methods for the Social Sciences: Honoring Human Experience* by Braud and Anderson (1998).

By locating this work in the context of this new transpersonal research, this dissertation may be recognized and affirmed as a work honoring unique, subjective human experience; in this specific case, a series of archetypal waking dream experiences.

As Braud and Anderson state,

> Transpersonal psychology seeks to honor human experience in its fullest and most transformative expression. It is usually identified as the "fourth face" in psychology with psychoanalytic, behavioristic, and humanistic psychologies as its historical predecessors. Transpersonal psychology seeks to delve into the most profound aspects of human experience, such as mystical and unitive experiences, personal transformative and meditative awareness, experience of wonder and ecstasy, and alternative and expansive states of consciousness. (p. xxi)

I would add yet another type of psychology to these mentioned: archetypal psychology. This is another way of describing the nature of this dissertation. Archetypes appeared in my waking dreams as teachers, priests, healers, shamans, little child, Wisdom and Holy Spirit, imparting their unique energy to the dreaming body. They then aligned with specific body chakras to heal, energize and transform. To me, these experiences fall under the Braud definition of exceptional human experience (EHE) because they occurred when the "experience relates to and is connected with the knowledge and its sources in a transformative way. Exceptional experiences (EE's) spotlight new areas of the unknown to be explored. Exceptional human experiences (EHE's) are experiences of dynamic interaction and connection with that unknown" (Braud and Anderson, 1998, p. 129).

Certainly, the experiences described in this dissertation fall under the stated purview of transpersonal research. Because of the many ways it conforms to the many examples of research specifically described in Braud and Anderson, this work fits the transpersonal research model. It is a relief to find a place where my exceptional human experiences are recognized and affirmed.

CHAPTER 1

INTRODUCTION

Chronic physical pain dominated my life in the late 1980s. Using Biogenics learned at the Shealy Pain Clinic, I began an extraordinary holistic recovery which far exceeded relief from physical pain. This study explores my seven year healing journey (1988-1995) that was mediated by spontaneous waking dreams.

Years after the onset of these waking dreams, I began studying archetypes, the chakra energy system of the body, and the power of imaging. As extraordinary as it seemed at the time, I began to suspect that through waking dreams I was accessing archetypal images which interacted synergistically with the chakra energy system of the body to manifest healing/wholeness/individuation. This study chronicles my seven-year healing journey and analyzes and discusses this experience as the interplay of archetypes acting upon the chakra energy system of my body. It may at times sound like fantasy, but I can only bear witness to what I experienced and what I know.

John Sanford (1992), a Jungian analyst and Episcopal priest wrote:

Sometimes our illness is an integral part of the process of individuation. Some illnesses persist until we have been led to a certain spiritual destination or goal: Then, they are alleviated in such a way that, as a result of our search for healing, we have become entirely new and more whole people. (p. 120)

This, indeed, is what happened to me. The astounding power of the images in these waking dreams and the amazing gifts of grace they bestowed brought healing to my mind, body, spirit, personal situations and relationships during those seven years, and the healing continues today. Once I committed to my journey to heal, I was held in the hand of the Divine. This was and continues to be my experience.

BACKGROUND OF THE STUDY

It was becoming more evident each day. I was dying and the indications were that it would be a long miserable process. Over the past few years, I had been x-rayed, tested, poked, prodded, analyzed, adjusted, and manipulated, and I still hurt all over, was constantly fatigued, was horribly depressed, and generally felt like I was under siege physically, emotionally, and spiritually. I considered suicide.

Allopathic medicine had not worked very well for me. Any relief I received came from alternative treatments; acupuncture and chiropractic treatments helped in the short term. It was a medical doctor practicing clinical ecology who finally diagnosed Epstein-Barr virus. The other diagnoses included osteoporosis and osteoarthritis, fibromyalgia, systemic candidiasis, fibrocystic breast disease, and an array of allergies, one of which was an allergy to estrogen. This caused a severe estrogen deficiency. One medical doctor pronounced, "You have an 80-year-old back," when I was 55 years old. Another predicted that, "You will be in a wheelchair in a year. It won't decrease the pain, unfortunately." Another looked very sober and informed me that, "When we see an endocrine deficiency this severe, we sometimes see that patient slide over the edge, and it is a long road back."

Gradually, by following a very strict diet and nystatin therapy prescribed by the clinical ecologist, I began to improve. I lost 40 pounds very quickly. That was a welcomed side effect I had not anticipated. Very slowly, I improved in some areas; however, the chronic pain was getting worse. Stress on the job had increased during the years, so I was also considering a career change or retirement. Amazingly, I had been able to drag through the day and keep teaching at a local community college. The effort to keep going, however, had taken an immense toll.

In 1987, my minister handed me a brochure from Shealy Comprehensive Pain and Stress Management Clinic in Springfield, Missouri, and I entered the clinic in May 1988. The Shealy Clinic, founded in 1971 by Dr. C. Norman Shealy, an internationally recognized physician (neurosurgeon), was the first comprehensive pain and stress management clinic in the country. I was a patient there for three weeks. During this time my treatment centered on Biogenics, a self-regulation program for pain management developed by Dr. Shealy which helps one to achieve physical, mental, and spiritual well-being, largely without drugs. Biogenics, based on biofeedback and autogenics, combines autosuggestion techniques, mental and spiritual exercises. According to studies involving the Biogenics training program, it has been helpful in treating the most serious chronic pain problems (Shealy, 1986). I practiced Biogenics several hours each day while at the clinic. Thus began my journey and my story.

Returning home from the Shealy Pain Clinic, I followed all of the treatment plan outlined by the doctors: proper diet, exercise, vitamin and mineral supplementation based on laboratory testing, and the Biogenics program. I was on no pain medication except buffered aspirin. For a very short period, I did the different relaxation and reprogramming exercises with the aid of the tapes made by the Shealy staff. During that time I was conscious of many physical sensations produced by the exercises. Some tapes concentrated on bringing warmth into the painful areas, while others concentrated on being aware of energy flowing through painful spots. Another exercise taught how to expand the energy field around the body, and one tape taught how to achieve spiritual attunement. Each of the many tapes taught a specific skill, and I became proficient enough that I was not dependent on the tapes. All through this time, I was experiencing the gift of the imagery while I was learning the various techniques.

From the beginning the results were varied and promising: less pain, less depression, and definite feelings of physical, psychological, and spiritual well-being. I was already feeling more relaxed and optimistic. I knew intuitively that this was the appropriate program for me. I liked the feeling of empowerment that came with learning how to heal from the inside out. I appreciated how nurturing it felt to care for myself. I liked having control over my healing time, the setting, and the comfort level. I believed that this investment of time and energy would pay dividends as long as I lived. And, of course, there were no insurance forms to file, no doctor's appointments to keep, and no drugs to remember to take. Most important, I was moving slowly out of the victim mind set.

During my Biogenics session, I followed a specific routine: I set aside a block of uninterrupted time. I positioned myself as comfortably as possible in a quiet room, and sometimes I lit a candle or played some soothing music. With my eyes closed I prayed a simple prayer of preparation and protection, giving thanks for the opportunity to accept the healing that my Creator willed for me.

As I continued this routine every day, the Biogenics sessions were dominated by waking dreams and/or audible messages with no image. Sometimes the waking dreams and audible messages came as little parables. Always, they were instructive, energizing, inspiring, and healing. Sometimes, I felt tingling or warmth in parts of my body; little bursts of electricity ran up along my spine. I kept a written record of all the images and messages given to me because I knew intuitively that they were critical to my healing even if I did not understand them in terms of content and process. Over the seven-year healing period, I collected more than 500 entries.

Detailed and complicated waking dreams continued to carry a definite, immediate, and numinous quality. This experience was unlike any other experience I had ever had, and needless to say, it piqued my interest. I wanted to understand what the waking dreams meant and how they related to the healing process I was experiencing. I needed help. I had not worked with images, had never heard of archetypes except in a superficial way, and had done little work with dreams. I certainly had never heard of chakras.

A friend of mine recommended that I see Len Evans, an Episcopal priest trained in Jungian psychology. I began meeting regularly with him. He was a wonderfully skilled, wise spiritual companion who introduced me to the world of dreams, intuition, archetypes, and myself.

In 1994 I started to find material on chakras. Although I understood only a portion of the technical material, I read all I could find on the subject. I began to receive regular energy treatments from Sam Winters. They were beneficial, but my understanding of how they worked was limited; however, I knew intuitively that I wanted to learn more. In 1995 my intuition led me to the Vision, Creativity and Intuition workshops led by C. Norm Shealy and Caroline Myss and I "came home." I learned at the first workshop that intuition is an innate quality and capability, specific for each person. It serves as guide, counselor and informer. As a segment of the Universal Mind, all knowing and manifestations are derived from intuition. Each and all bodily cells and systems respond to its direction. I was beginning to understand just how important intuition had been in my healing journey.

STATEMENT OF THE PROBLEM

Through spiritual mentoring and independent reading and reflection, I began to realize that the imagery (that is, the content) of the waking dreams which regularly occurred during the biogenic sessions was archetypal, that archetypes can relate to physical, psychological, and spiritual states of being, and that they have the creative power to heal. The more I learned about the body's chakra energy system and its relationship to total human functioning, the more I wondered if the archetypal images had interacted with my body's chakra energy system to generate the holistic healing I experienced.

When I tried to learn about chakra and archetype alignment and integration I found limited information. Wauters (1997) stated that chakras help identify where personal energy is blocked and that archetypes show which personal attitudes or emotional issues need to be addressed, so one can move to a higher level of consciousness. Jamal (1987) stated that the experience of an archetype aligning with an energy center can cause an instantaneous shift in perception and belief which makes it possible to reframe or unlearn limitations and negative perceptions and instantaneously re-program. According to

Braden (1997), to *become* requires a shift in viewpoint. Changing body chemistry by shifting viewpoints is perhaps the single most powerful tool available to people for the remainder of their lives. Although these writers acknowledge the possibility of healing through chakras and archetype integration, I found no record of ongoing holistic healing generated by archetypal imaging and its effect on the chakra energy system.

RESEARCH QUESTION

With seven years of documented waking dreams which detailed my healing journey, I wanted to see if the information I had acquired concerning images, archetypes and chakras could provide insight and greater understanding for the healing I had received prior to the new learning. My specific research question was this: Is it possible to track the interaction of the archetypal images on my body's chakra energy system accessed through Biogenics with the holistic healing I experienced? The purpose of this study was to answer that question.

SIGNIFICANCE OF THE STUDY

This study has both theoretical and applied significance. It offers testimonial evidence of the holistic healing power of a Biogenics program routinely practiced; it documents the content and process of the waking dreams experience; and it offers a theoretical explanation for the healing process through the interplay of archetypes on the chakra energy system which may open new lines of investigation in the study of archetype and chakra integration. For practitioners, it suggests another avenue to pursue for the total integration of clients' mental, physical, spiritual energy system to achieve improved health and individuation.

DEFINITION OF TERMS

The conceptual underpinnings of this paper, Biogenics, archetypes, chakras, and the integration of the chakra energy system and archetypes, are defined and discussed in the Literature Review. Terms used in this paper which may need clarification are included in this section.

Ego — The rational and central forces of conscious life; what gets us around in the world. Ego is the "I" or "executive" of the conscious personality (Sanford, 1995).

Personal unconscious — The personal layer of the unconscious, distinct from the collective unconscious; contains lost memories, repressed material, subliminal perceptions and other contents that are not yet ready for consciousness (Sharp, 1991).

Collective unconscious — Genetically inherited level of the mind. A vast mental reservoir of ideas, symbols, themes, and archetypes that form the raw material of most of the world's myths, legends, and religious systems (Fontana, 1994).

Libido — Energy which animates both the conscious and unconscious; also called psychic energy by Jung (Stein, 1998).

Transcendent Function — Jung concluded that, on the basis of his experiences with and observation of patients, beyond the conscious mind and the personal unconscious mind, there exists a realm of unconscious contents which transcends one's own individual experience. By touching this powerful and vital realm, one can transcend limitations and ego consciousness and come into contact with divine reality. Jung then concluded that if one's psyche could be viewed as a bridge between this transcendent power and one's physical body, healing — that is, healing from a religious source—could be experienced. (Kelsey, 1991)

Psyche — The totality of all psychological processes, both conscious and unconscious. The psyche is far from being a homogenous unit — on the contrary, it is a mass of contradictory impulses, inhibitions, and feelings (Sharp, 1991).

Intuition — The natural state of all living being: When it is not blocked, it is an instinct. All information needed for survival and for solutions to problems or for activation of creativity are available in the collective unconscious or in the morphogenic field. The challenge is to learn how to access that information. Any magnetic attraction which keeps us attached to past time and/or any psychological hang-ups are impediments to clear intuition. Intuition is the ability to see clearly in *present* time. Ways in which intuition may be enhanced and archetypes activated include: dream work, body work, walking meditation, deep relaxation, colored lights and glasses, good music, vigorous exercise, Chi Kung, some homeopathy, journaling, poetry, yogi breathing, and many sounds (Shealy and Myss, 1995).

According to Sharp (1991), in Jung's model of typology, intuition, like sensation, is an irrational function because its apprehension of the world is based on the perception of given facts. Unlike sensation, however, it perceives via the unconscious and is not dependent on concrete reality.

> In intuition a content presents itself whole and complete, without our being able to explain or discover how this content came into existence. Intuition is a kind of instinctive apprehension, no matter what contents ... Intuitive knowledge possesses an intrinsic certainty and conviction. Intuition may receive information from within (for instance, as a flash of insight of unknown origin) or be stimulated by what is going on in someone else. (p. 77)

Finally, a quote from a favorite small book of fiction, *The Alchemist* by Paulo Coelho (1998).

> The boy was beginning to understand that intuition is really a sudden immersion of the soul into the universal current of life, where the histories of all people are connected, and we are able to know everything, because it's all written there. (p. 76)

Individuation — Individuation is the process of integration or becoming a whole person. It is the result of a lived dialogue between the conscious and unconscious (both harmony and friction). An indestructible whole is forged out of the coincidence of opposites. The movement into the wholeness of one's personality as the union with God deepens is called spiritual individuation.

The process of individuation is one of evolution of individual consciousness in which the unconscious archetypal driving forces are integrated with consciousness. This process involves coming to terms with or dialoguing with the archetype (Shealy and Myss, 1993). Sharp (1991) asserts that the goal of the individuation process is the synthesis of the self. In Jung's view, no one is ever completely individuated. While the goal is wholeness and a healthy working relationship between the conscious and unconscious, the true value of individuation lies in what happens on the journey.

Soul — That within us that connects our consciousness to our inner depths. The soul's primary function is relationship, and the relationship between the ego and the inner world is the most important relationship of all, for if this is broken, relationships with other people and God are impossible. For a person to have a soul, he or she must relinquish egocentric identification with the outer mask and must be willing to free what is within. Soul is a biblical word rather than a contemporary psychological term (Sanford, 1992).

Spirit — According to Crowther, et al (1995), spirit equals a person's mind or feelings as distinct from body: a person's soul. Myss (1996) writes about coming to a realization that she was never taught in school, the fact that spirit is very much a part of daily life, it "embodies our thoughts and emotions and it records every one of them, from the most mundane to the visionary" (p. 3). She realized that spirit is the conscious force that is life itself. In Kavanaugh and Rodriguez (1979) Teresa of Avila states that there is a difference between spirit and soul but that the difference is so subtle as that of a spiritual marriage; different, yet one. May (1992) writes that spirit means "a vital dynamic force of being, that which is given by God and brings the soul into living reality" (p. 7). Spirit implies energy and power. By contrast, soul reflects the essence of one's existence; the whole living being.

Persona — One of Jung's primary archetypes. According to Sharp (1991), it is the I, usually the ideal aspects of ourselves, that we present to the world. Originally the word meant a mask worn by actors to indicate the role they played. "On this level, it is both a protective covering and an asset in mixing with other people" (p. 97).

Anima — One of Jung's primary archetypes. The inner feminine side of a man. "The anima is both a personal complex and an archetypal image of women in the male psyche" (Sharp, 1991, p. 18).

Animus — One of Jung's primary archetypes. The inner masculine side of a woman. "Like the anima, the animus is both a personal complex and an archetypal image" (Sharp, 1991, p. 23).

CHAPTER 2

LITERATURE REVIEW

Practice of the Biogenics technique induced the waking dreams which were filled with archetypal symbols or imagery. This study considers the possibility that these archetypal images interacted with the body's chakra system to accomplish the holistic healing I experienced. In this chapter the conceptual underpinnings of this study are discussed. Included in this review are the concepts of Biogenics, waking dreams, symbol, archetype in general and specific archetypes, the chakra system, and chakra-archetype integration.

BIOGENICS

Biogenics (*bio* 'life,' *genics* 'to produce') is a comprehensive multi-faceted self-regulation technique for the management of pain and stress which helps to achieve physical, mental and spiritual well-being, largely without drugs. It was developed by C. Norm Shealy, M.D., Ph.D. as a safe, natural alternative to surgery and chemical pain treatment (Shealy, 1985).

Biofeedback, a key component of Biogenics, has proven effective as a direct tool for self-regulation of a variety of diseases and internal functions. It is also useful in learning to enter both a state of relaxation and a state of reverie. Biofeedback's most powerful learning principle is that its practice gives immediate indication of how well it works by how the patient is feeling (Shealy, 1988).

Another key component of Biogenics is based on Psycho-synthesis, a comprehensive psychology developed by Dr. Roberto Assagioli, an Italian psychotherapist who was a colleague of Jung and Freud. Assagioli believed that his approach brought together personality and spirituality. His work sought to merge scientific elements of psychology with elements of mysticism to create a dynamic, integrated understanding of human nature and behavior. His work is known especially for how it helps to develop awareness of the higher, inner Self. Rocke de Coppens (1994) writes that Assagioli was said to have declared, "The only way out of human problems is the way up, to connect with the spiritual Self. Below, in lower states of consciousness, there are no solutions, above, in higher states of consciousness, there are no problems" (p. 53).

Autosuggestion, as developed by Emil Coue, is another important component of Biogenics. Coue based his theory on the premise that the will always yields to the imagination; that the language of the autonomic nervous system is imagery which is accessed through relaxation and that logic does not run the body, but rather pictures run the body (Shealy, 1988).

Briefly stated, components of Biogenics include: deep relaxation, belief in the possibility of health, positive attitude, physiological balancing techniques, emotional detachment, specific goals and spiritual attunement.

WAKING DREAMS

Ira Progoff in Campbell (1986) speaks of the waking dream in these terms:

> The term 'waking' is used not so much to indicate
> a contrast with dreams of sleep as to convey the large-

ness of the dream dimension. Dreams are not restricted to the physical condition of sleep. They pertain rather to the symbolic dimension of human experience as a whole. Thus, dreams may occur in sleep where we are accustomed to look for them; in waking states where we find ourselves living out the symbolic aspect of life; and in twilight states that are between the state of sleeping and waking.

Dreaming in all three of these conditions expresses an underlying quality, not only of human existence but of the nature of the human psyche. This is specifically the quality of the psyche that unfolds in terms of symbols, which may be either symbolic imagery, symbolic experience, or intuitive perception of the symbolic meaning of life. All these together constitute the symbolic dimension of human experience. (p. 177)

Kelsey (1981) writes about a form of waking dreams or visions, in which the dream images are intruded into the waking consciousness. The images are no different from those that can be experienced during sleep, except that they reach the field of consciousness during periods of wakefulness. They arise as spontaneously and with as little ego control as the dream, and in most cases the visions are involuntary.

Poet Rainer Maria Rilke is quoted in Fox (1983) regarding the value and importance of the image:

You must give birth to your images. They are the future waiting to be born ... fear not the strangeness you feel. The future must enter into long before it happens .... Just wait for the birth ... for the hour of new clarity. (p. 201)

SYMBOL

For centuries, philosophers, psychologists and religious thinkers have recognized innate universal animating images, called archetypes, which guide human behavior at an unconscious level. "When the archetype manifests itself in the here and now of space and time, it can be perceived in some form by the conscious mind. Then, we speak of a symbol" (Whitmont, 1991, p. 119). The waking dreams I experienced were rich in archetypal symbols. In this literature review both symbol and archetypes are discussed.

Jung is quoted in Cirlot (1971): "The psychic mechanism that transforms energy is the symbol" (p. xxxv). Edinger (1992) asserts that *symbol* comes from the Greek, and it combines two root words: sym, meaning together or with, and bolon, that which has been thrown. In original Greek usage, "symbol referred to two halves of an object such as a stick or a coin which two parties broke between them as a pledge and to later prove the identity of the presenter of the one part to the holder of the other" (p. 130). Psychologically speaking, the symbol leads us to the missing part of the whole man. It relates to our original totality. It heals our split, our alienation from life.

Edinger (1992) states further:

Symbols are spontaneous products of the archetypal psyche. One cannot manufacture a symbol, one can only discover it. Symbols are carriers of psychic energy. This is why it is proper to consider them as something alive. They transmit to the ego, either consciously or unconsciously, life energy which supports, guides and motivates the individual. The archetypal psyche is constantly creating a steady stream of living symbolic imagery. (p. 110)

In order to appear as a symbol it must, in other words, have an archetypal ground plan. But, an archetype is not necessarily identical with a symbol. It is always a potential symbol, and its dynamic nucleus is ready to actualize itself and manifest itself as a symbol. All such diverse phenomenon as instinct responses, ideas, affects, emotions, behavioral habits, complexes, symptoms, and symbolic experiences are aspects or manifestation of the same process, the actualization of archetypes (Whitmont, 1991).

Kelsey (1991) believes that when men forget how to think in symbols or symbolically, the symbols in dreams become a closed book. Men forget that these images describe realities that influence the human psyche. Thinking symbolically is very different from the rational, analytical thinking that Descartes helped to define for the modern world. Symbolic thinking is thinking through images, through imagination. It has its own meanings, its own direction and way, which can be understood by the rational, conscious mind. Thus it is the basis of many scientific discoveries, as well as being the language of literature and art. It is symbolic thinking that also produces religious writings and is used in many meditative exercises. When men learn to think symbolically, they will not only understand the language of dreams, of art and literature, but they will also understand sacred scripture and texts.

Myss (1996) teaches that learning how to see in a symbolic way ("symbolic sight") is a way of seeing and understanding self, others, and life events in terms of archetypal patterns. Learning to use this sight teaches a healthy objectivity that brings out the symbolic meaning of events, people, and the challenges of life — especially the painful, confusing challenges of illness and disease. Developing symbolic sight gives a way to see into the spirit and the limitless potential for healing and wholeness. Ultimately, with practice and intentionality, symbolic sight will yield the ability to use intuition to interpret the power of symbols in life.

ARCHETYPES

For centuries thinkers from various disciplines have tried to explicate the form and function of archetypes, the innate, universal animating images which unconsciously guide human behavior. The language used to express this idea has differed by discipline and has evolved over time.

While the term archetype is usually associated with the theories of C. G. Jung, Jung points out in Hoeller (1989) that:

> ... the term occurs as early as Philo Judaeus with reference to the Imago Dei (God image) in man. It can be found in Iraneus who stated, "The Creator of the world did not fashion these things directly from himself but copied them from archetypes outside himself .... In the Corpus Hermeticum God is called ... 'archetypal light' ... for our purpose this term ... tells us that ... we are dealing with archaic or — I would say — primordial types, that is, with universal images that have existed since remote times" (p. 3).

Cirlot (1971) defines archetypes as both sources of energy and patterns of energy. They are like all-embracing parables: their meaning is only partially accessible. Their deepest significance remains a secret which existed long before man himself and reaches far beyond man.

Campbell (1959) notes that while Jung's idea of the archetype is one of the leading theories recognized today, it was a development of the earlier theories of several others, including Adolph Bastain. Bastain recognized, as he traveled widely, the similarity of what he termed "elementary ideas" of mankind. He called that similarity by the term "ethnic ideas" for the ways in which these ideas are differently articulated and elaborated in the physical, local manifestation of these universal forms. Bastain assumed that there is in the structure and functioning of the psyche a certain degree of spontaneity and consequent uniformity throughout the history and domain of the human species — an order of psychological laws inherent in the structure of the body which "has not radically changed since the period of the Aurignacian caves and can be as readily identified in the jungles of Brazil as in the cafes of Paris, as readily in the igloos of Baffin Land as in the harems of Marrakech" (Campbell, 1959, p. 33).

According to Henry (1992), Jung maintained that

… the archetypes that shape consciousness by regulating, modifying and motivating, act like instinct. It is therefore natural to suppose that these factors are connected with instincts, and to ask whether the typical situations which these collective principles constitute are not actually identical with patterns of behavior — instincts. Jung has suggested that "instinct and archetype are two ends of an activity spectrum that is not concerned with reason, but which nevertheless guide the human." The true content, Jung further maintains, of all myth, religion and "isms" is archetypal. (p. 53)

Taylor (1992) believes that it was Jung's contribution to recognize the positive regulatory aspect of the processes of instincts and to emphasize the link between the physiology of instinct and individual and group thought processes. When we meet archetypal energies in the dream world, or in waking life, with courage, imagination, and a willingness to sacrifice immediate interests for the love and benefit of others, this decision has its effect on the archetypal energies, as well as on the individual consciousness that enters into the engagement. It is also true that when humans struggle with personal, separate dramas, collective archetypal energies are given shape and made manifest.

> Just as the archetypal energies which come from the collective unconscious provide the foundation of both the dreaming and waking world, so the waking and dreaming experience of human beings (and other vital organisms) become the arena where those archetypal energies are given vitality, made concrete, acted out, and allowed to evolve and change. As they are 'made flesh' the archetypal energies are, in turn, woven back into the myths and the dreams, echoing back into the transpersonal realm that Jung called the collective unconsciousness or the objective psyche. (Taylor, 1992, p. 250)

Raine in Bancroft (1989) speaks of archetypes and symbols in a refreshingly poetic manner. She speaks of them as being buried gold deep in our subconscious.

> They come, not as allegory but rather as epiphanies; awe inspiring glimpses that move us deeply and inexplicably. These images seem put into our hands like clues which we are invited to follow back and back, for they draw us irresistibly, as if by magic; and this is no less so when we encounter them in nature than in dreams or visions. By their numinous nature, we recognize them: and not with academic curiosity do we

pursue them to their mysterious source, but as we follow the beloved person unable to get away .... They arise as living impulses, urges of our own being and therefore compelling. We cannot rest until we have followed them to their sources, or as far as our understanding allows. (p. 71)

From Henry (1992) comes this interesting clinical view:
An explosion of neuroanatomical and neuroendocrine research during the past decade has given a physical basis of the maternal and gender typical patterns of behavior known to the analytical psychologist as archetypes, to the mythologist as Gods and Goddesses, and to the ethologist as instincts. (p. 281)

From Robert R. Leichtman (Leichtman and Japakse, 1989) comes this fresh and unique perspective:
Divine intelligence is not just a huge cosmic brain. It is a force field of intelligence filled with living dynamic energies. The energies are what are called 'archetypal forces.' They are the abstract forces from which every thing that is has been created. Love, wisdom, and power are the three most basic of these forces. Others are grace, joy, peace, beauty, harmony, and abundance. When we have a problem, it is a sign that we lack one of these archetypal forces, or are misusing it (p. 67)

Finally, Shealy (1995) makes these personal observations about archetypes:
We perceive that each soul agrees to a cluster of archetypes prior to birth to encounter in an educational relationship. This cluster is a dynamic force

which provides the situations and emotional encounters for growth of individual consciousness toward a transcendent understanding of the unity of all beings within an holistic holographic system. Understanding archetypes provides a deep sophisticated philosophical insight into personal reality. Each personal sacred contract is very individual but has in common with all others the *wise, responsible, loving use of power.* A foundational triad of archetypes takes the leading role with others playing roles at varying times and with varying intensity. (p. 3)

According to Shealy and Myss (1995), the fundamental role of the archetype is to teach its highest ideals (from tribal to spiritual). Ideally, each archetype ultimately evolves into spirituality, and virtually any archetype may teach the highest spiritual lesson, depending on the maturity level of the archetype. Archetypes change and evolve constantly: They carry vital kinetic energy.

Each archetype has a dark or shadow side and sometimes the only way necessary lessons may be learned is through the messages carried by the energies of the shadow. Shadow archetypes represent qualities that are thought to be unworthy or immoral. By rejecting these qualities a split is created in the psyche that must be healed if wholeness is to be achieved. Unrecognized and neglected, the shadow cannot be integrated into the total personality and will consequently be dropped into the unconscious and cause unconscious reactions and behaviors that do not help the individuation process. In truth, the shadow is a teacher whose goal is to enlighten and assist.

By way of illustration, consider the shadow prostitute

archetype. This archetype is recognized by the popular concept that, "Everyone has a price." Anytime moral, ethical beliefs are violated, the prostitute may be at work; paradoxically, since the ultimate goal is to allow the archetype to guide towards the highest potential, the spiritual ideal of the prostitute is the sacrosanct, the incorruptible, which *is the* highest potential of that archetype.

Another way of understanding the role of these universal patterns of behavior, again according to Shealy and Myss (1995), is to consider the unique aspects of the concept of archetypal integration. For instance, broad representations of "spirit" according to Jung, may be manifested as mother, father, sage, crone, god, goddess, child, magician, doctor, priest, teacher, professor, grandfather, etc. In other words, "when emotionally perceived as the spirit, virtually any archetype may ultimately provide the transcendent message" (p. 6).

SPECIFIC ARCHETYPAL IMAGES (SYMBOLS)

The waking dreams I experienced using the Biogenics technique were filled with recurring and/or significant archetypal symbols. Each archetypal symbol has a commonly understood meaning which is summarized in the following discussions.

Archetype: The Journey

Cirlot (1971) writes that from the spiritual point of view, the journey is never merely a passage through space, but rather an expansion of the urgent desire for discovery and change that underlies the actual movement and expansion of traveling; hence, to study, to inquire, to seek, or to live with intensity through new and profound experiences are all modes of traveling or are spiritual and symbolic equivalents of the journey. The true life journey is neither acquiescence or escape; it is evolution.

Campbell (1959) observed that the most universal archetypal dynamic is that of the journey. It is the Hero's journey, which can be a picture of the process of growth. He called it the monomyth. Very briefly stated:

The Hero (ego) leaves home (earth mother, tribe, etc.), receives counsel from wise old men or women (crone, sage, wizard, or inner wisdom, etc.), faces some great evil or challenge (dragon, evil, new ideas, illness, injury), returns a wounded healer with life- giving message (new consciousness) or is killed and reborn. Thus, the hero is a carrier of consciousness.

Pearson (1991) asserts,

When we take our journey and come back to share what we have learned, we help transform much more than our own lives. Inevitably, we find others like ourselves who have found similar truths. We are lonely only when we are conforming or hiding and not sharing what we know with others. When we have the courage to be who we are — to see what we see, know what we know, and act on that knowledge — we can find others like ourselves. And then together we can begin creating new worlds. (p. 281)

Harner writes in Doore (1988), "No one is better qualified to understand the messages of the journey than the person who is undertaking it, and also that those messages are perfectly formed for the journeyer in question" (p. 182).

The healing journey is both a psychological and spiritual journey, a journey back to the Spirit. The art of healing becomes a sacred journey of the soul back to God, its source and its wholeness.

Archetype: My Path

One of the constants in my images was that I was on My Path when the images began. Nottingham (1993) writes that, psychologically speaking, the path is like a great stream of archetypal images and universal patterns of consciousness. Myths and parables that resonate in us are the ones which are attuned to this great psychic roadway. Nottingham believes that in the Divine Plan for spiritual evolution toward co-creativity, the path is formed by universal images that exist in the unconscious of each soul. These images operate like road markers to give us feedback that we are on the right path. They also contain a mystery or a creative tension which provides the energy to move on and evolve further.

On any path or road, a bridge spans something which interrupts its use, and the bridge becomes a part of the way. At the end of my seven years, this is what happened to me. The path can be defined as a movement in consciousness upward or inward; that is, from involvement in dense forms to those of greater freedom and beauty. My Path symbolizes both freedom and beauty, purpose and destination.

This following concept of the path is found in Andrews (1997). The ancient Hebrew mystics used a powerful application of the creative imagination in a technique they called Pathworking. The paths depicted in the Qabalistic Tree of Life are symbolic pathways to various levels of the mind and the universe. They link different levels of the mind (Sefirot) and the energies available to us at those levels, employing powerful symbols in imaginative scenarios to invoke and manifest specific energies into the individual's life. It is a reminder that the Tree of Life and all of its energies are within.

From Gibran (trans. 1971), "Say not that 'I have found the path of the soul!' Say rather, 'I have met the soul walking upon my path' " (p. 55).

Archetype: The Self or self

In Sharp (1991) is found this definition of Self: "The archetype of wholeness and the regulating center of the psyche; a transpersonal power that transcends the ego" (p. 119). This archetype may appear in dreams in many guises: as king, hero, prophet, savior, or as a totality symbol such as a circle, square, cross, etc. Experiences of the Self carry a numinous quality that is characteristic of spiritual revelations. Hence, "Jung believed that there was no essential difference between the Self as an experiential, psychological reality and the traditional concept of a supreme deity. It might equally be called the 'God within us' " (p. 120).

Another aspect of self is provided by Clift and Clift (1992). Self is sometimes manifested in dreams by the disembodied voice, like a voice of God, which pronounces some statement to the dreamer. Sometimes brief, often with no visual image, but there is no doubt about the message. It is very direct; these messages should be taken seriously. Jung considered the self to be the prime archetype, the one from which all others ultimately come. The self is transcendent. It is not equal to the ego. To say that someone is self-centered is to say that one is precisely *not* egotistical and is not easily knocked off center. "When we single-handily ally our egos with the desires and activities of the self, we are granted a new freedom to walk along paths in life that were formerly barred to us" (p. 117).

In Stein (1998) is found this explanation and discussion.

Wholeness is said to result when the self is realized in consciousness. Jung's version of living in Tao is when wholeness is practiced on a regular basis. Although wholeness seems at first sight to be nothing but an abstract idea, it is nevertheless empirical in so far as it is anticipated by the psyche in the form of spontaneous or autonomous symbols. These are the quarternity or mandala symbols, which occur in dreams of all people of all epochs of history. The self, a transcendent non-psychological entity acts on the psychic system to produce symbols of wholeness.

Archetype: Number Seven — Seven Years

Sanford (1995) asserts that the number seven is considered to be a sacred number. In Christianity and Hinduism it is the number of God, the mystical number. The number seven in dreams may be a symbol for risk, opportunity, and inner transformation. According to St. Augustine, in Sanford (1995) "the number seven signified the Holy Spirit as well as the consummation of time. For there is a revolution of all time in seven days" (p. 334).

Blavatsky (2000) quotes from the German journal, *Die Gegenwart* on the significance of the number seven.

> The number seven was considered sacred not only by all the cultured nations of antiquity and the East, but was held in the greatest reverence even by the later nations of the West. The astronomical origin of this number is established beyond any doubt. Man, feeling himself time out of mind dependent upon the heavenly powers, ever and every where made earth subject to heaven. The largest and brightest of the luminaries thus became in his sight the most important and highest of powers; such even the planets which whole

antiquity numbered as seven. In course of time these were transformed into seven deities. The Egyptian had seven original and higher gods; the Phoenicians seven Kabiris; the Persians, seven angels opposed by seven demons and seven celestial abodes paralleled by seven lower regions. To represent more clearly this idea in its concrete form, the seven gods were often represented as one seven-headed deity. The whole heaven was subjected to the seven planets; hence, in nearly all religious systems we find seven heavens. (p. 1)

In medieval magic, seven was the most popular number of mystic power after three. It was often associated with the heavenly Seven Sisters, guardians of the axis mundi (Walker, 1988). The Bible contains many and varied references to the significance of the number seven. A few include:
Jacob served seven years for Rachel.
Creation was completed in seven days.
Feasts often lasted for seven days.
Fasts often lasted for seven days.
The number seven was a critical factor in visions and dreams, i.e., seven years of famine and feast, seven golden lamp stands, seven angels who had seven plagues. Social customs and rituals often involved the number seven, i.e., man served seven years for a wife, seven days of mourning, year of Jubilee (7 X 7 years) and the seven sayings from the cross.

Rain (1990) points out that some Native Americans believe that seven always has to do with the six spiritual forces that function within the physical body in conjunction with the body's own force: hence, the total of seven. Kelsey (1981) asserts that the spiritual growth process was envisioned by alchemists as a seven-rung ladder.

The Eastern concept of the seven chakras is vital to the understanding of our consciousness and how our energy system operates. All of our senses, all of our perceptions, all of our possible states of awareness, can be divided into seven categories, and each of these seven categories can be associated with one of the seven chakras. Each of the seven chakras is energy vibrating at a certain frequency in a logical and orderly sequence of seven vibrations (Bruyere, 1994).

According to Cirlot (1971):

> Seven is symbolic of spirituality, of perfect order, a complete period or cycle. It is comprised of the union of ternary and the quaternary, and hence is endowed with exceptional value. It corresponds to the seven directions of space (six existential dimensions plus the center) to the seven pointed star, to the reconciliation of the square with the triangle by superimposing the latter upon the former (as the sky over the earth). It is the number forming the basic series of musical notes, of colors, and of planetary spheres as well as of the gods corresponding to them, and also of the capitol sins and their opposing virtues. It also corresponds to the three dimensional cross, and finally, it is the symbol of pain. (p. 233)

After selecting a period of seven years as my period of time for this study, I found that, indeed, the seven years completed one cycle of movement and growth, then began a time of transition into another distinct cycle of growth and evolutionary change.

Archetype: The Poet

*Note: I have included this archetype as part of the litera-
ture review because of an experience I had during the process
of writing this dissertation, an experience which contributed to
the analysis of the dreams and results of the study. At one point
in writing this dissertation, I became stuck. I could not handle
all of the material-seven years is a long period of time, and I
seriously considered cutting the period of time or giving up the
dissertation all together. Then a most amazing thing happened. I began to write poetry, something I had never before
done. The words appeared on the paper and seemed familiar,
but they were in such interesting combinations. During a
period of five months, I was gifted with seventeen poems.
Then, I caught on! They were provided by the poet archetype.
Not only was I being gifted with a classic and timely example
of how archetypes work, but I was also given the clarity and
direction to proceed.*

The following discussion came from Hunter (1997) who
writes that the language of the poem is evidence that it arises
from a special mental state in which communication is of a
higher order then the poet's ordinary thinking or speech. "Dis-
parate thoughts come together in similes and metaphors
showing what they have in common; brief memories of past
insights come together with the urgency of the present
moment" (p. 32).

Poet William Blake said that inspiration surged so strongly
that he felt his long poems were being dictated to him by
divine will. He wrote a poem in 1802 from immediate dicta-
tion. Twenty or thirty lines came at a time, without thinking
and even somewhat against his will.

Many cultures have created poetry to express mystical
insight and to expand the capacity for higher consciousness.

There seems to be a very close association between mysticism and poetry; in the Eskimo language the word for poetry derives from the same word as soul. Maritain called poetry "that intercommunication between the inner being of things and the inner being of the human Self which is a kind of divination" (Hunter, 1997, p. 33). "Plato called poetry coiled language because of its many layers of meaning" (Hunter, 1997, p. 34).

Archetype: Wise Ones

Fontana (1994) in *The Secret Language of Dreams* maintains that the Wise Man or Wise Woman are archetypes that Jung called the mana personality. They are symbols of a primal source of growth and vitality which can heal or destroy, attract or repel. They may appear as doctor, magician, professor, priest, teacher, father, mother, crone, sage, or any other authority figure. By their presence and teachings they convey a sense that higher states of consciousness are within the dreamer's grasp. Jung enjoyed a lifelong relationship with a mana personality named Philemon. It is said that he spent days talking to him.

According to Shealy and Myss (1995) this archetype is usually very old, very wise, and usually revered. Wisdom imparted is impartial and for the good of all. He or she symbolizes human wisdom that has not been damaged by too much education. The Wise One usually has to go through an initiation and usually must leave family or tribe to have wisdom activated. They must learn to be and stay non-ego identified, and they also must be able to learn from life experiences, especially from mistakes.

Edinger (1992) believes that wisdom is the attribute that the Wise Ones bring. Wisdom can be thought of as light in psychological terms; the Wise Ones bring the light of consciousness. The archetypal forces which are represented by the Wise Ones are bringers of themselves as gifts of the ego, reminding the individual of his/her suprapersonal connections. Critical connecting links between the ego and archetypal psyche, they transmit symbolic meaning.

Archetype — The Shaman

Achterberg (1985) discusses the shaman. The word *Shaman* derives from the Russian SAMAN. Weston La Barre, a Duke University professor of anthropology, notes that the shaman is the world's oldest professional, and the one from whom both the modern doctor and priest descend. The shaman was the original artist, dancer, musician, singer, dramatist, intellectual, poet, bard, ambassador, advisor of chiefs and kings, entertainer, actor and clown, magician, juggler, folksinger, weatherman, artisan, culture hero and trickster-transformer.

Achterberg (1985) notes that Mircea Eliade, an author of classic anthropological and theological works, has reviewed the vast literature and finds the shaman characterized as priest, magician, physician, sorcerer, exorcist, political leader, psychotic, and mountebank. The shaman "is defined both by practices and intention: Shamanic practice involves the ability to move in and out of a special state of consciousness, has a notion of a guardian spirit complex, and has the purpose of helping others" (p. 13).

Achterberg (1985) continues by pointing out that the wounded healer concept is closely associated with the shaman. This concept implies that some kind of personal transformation was produced as a result of some crisis which was encountered and transcended. This event pointed the shaman toward a mission and gifted him/her with unusual wisdom, especially knowledge of the worlds of the spirit. The shaman serves his/her healing vocation with this wisdom. It is the process of wounding or becoming a wounded healer via transformation that is most important to the shaman's calling.

The shaman's work is conducted in the realm of the imagination, and the shaman's expertise in using this realm for the benefit of the community has been recognized throughout recorded history. In fact, shamanism is the oldest and most widespread method of healing with the imagination. Archaeological evidence suggests that the techniques of the shaman are at least 20,000 years old. (p. 15)

In Doore (1988), Achterberg is quoted:

Imagery is the thought process that stimulates and uses the five senses: the mechanism that communicates between perception, emotion, and physiological change. Within this modality, we are not only better able to understand our needs and control our physiology, be we can reach planes beyond ourselves. Shamans have always understood that we need go nowhere but inside ourselves for our transformation. Dreams, visions, and other products of imagination are responsible for more of the world's information on health and disease than any other phenomenon. Imagination is recognized by many as the oldest and greatest of healing resources. (p. 122)

Achterberg continues by pointing out that sages and crones were shamans. They could determine the direction of their community life on many levels. The physicians in Greek medicine were shamans as were the wise women in the Middle Ages. They were healer-priests in Egypt. Today, persons in medicine, psychology, and religion may personify the shaman. Primarily, they are those who have a gift of great insight into the human condition, and who have attained wisdom concerning the realm of the spirit. Native populations still depend on the shaman, as they have for centuries, to be the holistic wounded healer-priest who serves their communities.

Mehl in Doore (1988) asserts that one reason that shamanic healing is unique is because the world view of the shaman is unique. Briefly stated:

- All parts of the world are interconnected on all levels.
- Objects observable to human senses are local manifestations of larger patterns of energy.
- That which is imperceptible to human senses is as important in illness as that which is measured through the senses.
- Consciousness is all pervasive: "everything is alive."
- The universe as a whole is sacred and has purpose and meaning.

Taylor (1992) writes that basic concepts, vocabulary and insights of the shaman are of particular value for today because they raise intuitive awareness, personal courage, and the awareness of beauty to the same importance as abstract theory and rational thought. Shaman energies raise and release one's own creative energies and those same energies are valuable in nurturing and transforming our communities. The basic theology of shamanism is always the same. Everything is alive in the dream.

Kelsey (1981) speaks of the need for modern day Christian shamans and the important role that these spiritual leaders fill in the Christian faith tradition. These modern shamans are desperately needed to guide people who are searching for a way to encounter the divine that will transform their lives. Because the shamans have dealt with the destructive side of reality, they have gone through the pain and evil and then have returned as wounded healers to help others.

Kelsey (1981) continues that the Christian ministers, like the native shaman, put people in touch with their holy experiences; concrete manifestations of the divine spirit. Articulate, compassionate and contemplative, this modern shaman must be willing to use his or her own pain to help others in their search for wholeness. "In a real sense, every Christian who allows the Spirit to move in him or her is a shaman" (p. 220).

THE CHAKRAS

Brofman (1998) states that *Chakra* is a Sanskrit word meaning wheel, or vortex, and refers to each of the energy centers that create our consciousness, our body's energy system. These seven (some believe there are eight or more) chakras or wheels function as pumps or valves, regulating the flow of energy throughout our energy system. The spinal cord contains six of the seven chakras in a pipe. They are placed at intervals that move energy from place to place through the whole canal.

Brofman (1998) continues with a discussion of the chakra system. The human body can be described as a system of overlapping and intertwined nervous, glandular, and skeletal networks that can be visually observed. But beyond these physical systems lies this network of energetic centers or energy anatomy. This energy anatomy influences health as profoundly as does physical anatomy. The aura is a part of this energy anatomy. The personal aura is generated by the spinning of the vortexes within the body. A personal energy field, or individual aura, is controlled by the chakras and reflects how one's life is actually lived: It mirrors the flow of the life. This auric field becomes more then the symbol for life. The aura is life. As our auric field or electromagnetic field is generated by the spinning of the chakras, the frequency determines the color of a particular chakra. In fact, each of these dynamic centers through which the energy is distributed has color, sound, and frequency.

According to Myss (1996), this energy anatomy with its seven chakras records and stores information about experiences, beliefs, and values. Specific chakras manage specific categories of information. Good, wise management of the energy centers leads to positive health and balance in daily functioning; however, poor management results in energy "leakages" that drain cells of vital life force, which leads to low self-esteem, disease, negative relationships, and general unwellness.

Chakras interact with the physical body in two major ways: the endocrine system and the nervous system. Each of the seven chakras is associated with one of the seven endocrine glands, and also with a group of nerves called a plexus. Each chakra is associated with a particular part of the physical body and particular function with the body controlled by that particular plexus or particular endocrine gland (Brofman, 1988).

Bruyere (1994) states that each of the chakras has a physical, an emotive, a creative, and a celestial component. Also, each has its own purpose or particular viewpoints based upon the area of consciousness that it influences. This area of consciousness is yet another component of the chakras. This component is simply an area or realm of existing or potential consciousness. "Each chakra can be said to have a 'prime directive.' It has purpose and a mind of its own; it is going somewhere" (p. 40).

Bruyere (1994) gives a historical perspective of energy systems: "In antiquity, before science and religion were divided, the chakras were an integrated part of life" (p. 26); an aspect of spiritual tradition and practice, and also a reflection of natural laws. They were at the root of the ancient sciences. At least 97 different cultures recognized the human energy system. All healers in these cultures knew about and understood the energetic body. Egyptians and Chinese, as well as the Hindus, Greeks, and the Native Americans, knew of the chakra system, although they called them by different names. Native Americans, according to their myths and lore which go back thousands of years, believed that the lower five chakras are aligned to the animal forms, i.e., the snake, the fish, the bird, the mammal, and man. The sixth is aligned with all spirits, living and dead. The seventh chakra is the Kachina, symbolizing the Universal Spirit, which they believe embodies all animate matter.

Again according to Bruyere (1994) Tehuty, an Egyptian priest-scribe, also known in myth as the Greek God Hermes, was first credited with defining the elementary nature of the chakra system some fifty-thousand-years ago. According to this ancient tradition, the progress up the chakras from the first to the seventh and their associated elements are fire, water, air, earth, ether, radium and magnatum. The element that each center represents becomes a reflection of what that chakra views life as being like, i.e., the first chakra views fire as life because the fire sparks the concept into being.

In the Chinese tradition, the oldest continuous civilization, life is considered to be the result of all important Chi. Chi in Chinese literally means gas or ether. It is their belief that Chi comes from the universe and flows through the body in channels or acupuncture meridians. The ancient Chinese saw Chi as breath in the body or the vital energy that animated the body. Acupuncture is the ancient technique for activating the electromagnetic system by using needles which, when inserted into the body's chemical reservoirs, generates or improves the flow of energy.

Bruyere (1994) continues: Through the ages, with the conquests of many of the ancient civilizations, vast libraries were burned and massive volumes of antiquarian and esoteric wisdom were destroyed. With the coming of the Dark Ages the only place, in many cultures, that these mysteries were preserved were by sacred priesthood where they were transmitted to initiates and through oral traditions as in the culture of the Native Americans. The Chinese, however, have practiced medicine based on the Chi or energy structure throughout the ages. "It has taken thousands of years, but within this century, scientists and spiritual seekers alike have once again begun to view the laws of nature and the laws of God as reflections of the same truth" (p. 27). It is this viewpoint that has allowed the scientific investigation into the chakra system and its implications to come back into the thinking of scientists, psychologists, counselors, physicians, and spiritual seekers everywhere. Gerber (2000) writes:

> Ancient approaches to understanding disease and body healing often viewed illness from the perspective of the human spirit, or the body's life-forming energy. These somewhat mystical viewpoints may now hold the key to understanding why people become ill and how they can regain their health. (p. 2)

Gerber identifies the part old, part new field of vibrational or energy medicine as a newly emerging field where ancient healing lore and the latest discoveries of science create a new approach to the diagnosis of disease — a synthesis of modern scientific insights into the energetic make-up of the body's atoms and molecules combined with mystical observations of the systems of the body that are critical but less well known or understood.

Myss (1996), in her ground breaking book *Anatomy of the Spirit*, takes a physiopsychospiritual view of power and energy and maintains that the nature of human energy is a science in itself. It is the science of creation. "The power that feeds our bodies, our minds, and our hearts does not originate in our DNA. Rather, it is rooted in Divinity itself. The truth is as simple as that" (p. 78).

Myss believes that each chakra "warehouses" a particular power. These ascend from the densest physical power (chakras one, two and three at the base of spine) to the most etheric or spiritual (four, five, six and seven ascending up the spine). The first three centers are attuned to the issues that concern us with physical and external power. The next four centers are attuned to nonphysical or internal power.

According to Myss (1996) each of the seven levels of power in our energy system contains a single sacred truth. "We are born with an inherent knowledge of these seven truths woven into our energy system. Violating these truths weakens our spirit and our physical body; honoring these truths enhances our spirit and our physical body" (p. 76). What drains spirit, drains body, drains power. What fuels spirit, fuels body, and builds power. Matter and spirit interact. Myss further believes that the common ingredient in every single energy dysfunction is an issue of power.

Myss (1996) identifies three truths common to the spiritual traditions of Hindu, Christian, and Judaica:

1. Misdirecting the power of one's spirit will generate consequences to one's body and life.
2. Every human being will encounter a series of challenges that will negatively affect one's physical power base, i.e., loss of wealth, health, loved ones, etc. This loss will activate a crisis of faith which will precipitate a search for deeper meaning and trigger psychological and spiritual "ascension" or individuation or wholeness.
3. "To heal from the misdirection of one's spirit, we must be willing to release the past, cleanse one's spirit and return to the present moment" (p. 76).

Carrying the integration of several faiths and the concept of the chakras and power further, Myss aligns the Seven Chakras, the Seven Sacred Truths, the Seven Christian Sacraments, and the Jewish Tree of Life Sefirot, creating a script not only for the development of our consciousness, but a spiritual language of healing as well as a map of the inevitable challenges in our holistic healing process.

Shealy (1999) maintains that the ultimate regulator of brain and mind, and thus, the electromagnetic energetic framework of life, is the human spirit and that fear, anger, guilt, anxiety, depression, pessimism, and greed sap our health by blocking the energy flow. He believes the antidotes are joy, laughter, happiness, serenity, peacefulness, optimism, forgiveness, patience, tolerance, compassion, love and a desire to do good and help others. These attributes of the spirit enhance health and well-being. The key to good health is attitude, that is, one's belief in the ultimate goodness of the universe. Relaxation, visualization, and meditation are some of the tools for developing critical spiritual values.

Figure 1
Location and Characteristics of Chakras,
Seven Sacred Truths and Christian Sacraments.

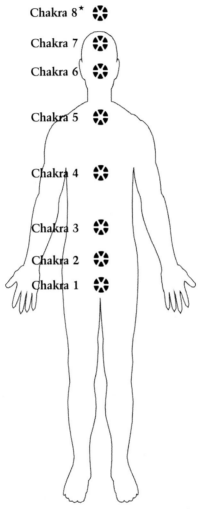

Chakra 8*

Chakra 7

Chakra 6

Chakra 5

Chakra 4

Chakra 3

Chakra 2

Chakra 1

*Not recognized widely, information incomplete
Illustration of Chakra Source: Caroline Myss, *Anatomy of the Spirit*,
Harmony Books, NY 1996

Chakra 8 *Center of Archetypal Power:* *
Location: Above head
Color: White

Chakra 7 *Center of Spiritual Power:* Connection to higher power
Location: Muscular and skeletal system, hair, skin, CNS
Psychological Issues: Values, faith, spirituality, inspiration
Color: Violet
Sacrament: Extreme Unction
Sacred Truth: Live in the Present Moment

Chakra 6 *Center of Mind Power:* Wisdom and intuition
Location: Brain, nervous system, eyes, nose, ears, pineal and pituitary glands
Psychological Issues: Self evaluation, truth, intellect, emotional intelligence
Color: Indigo
Sacrament: Ordination
Sacred Truth: Seek Only the Truth

Chakra 5 *Center of Will Power:* Will and choice
Location: Throat, neck, mouth, thyroid, hypothalmus
Psychological Issues: Choices, judgement, knowledge, expression of will
Color: Blue
Sacrament: Confession
Sacred Truth: Surrender Personal Will to Divine Will

Chakra 4 *Center of Emotional Power:* Forgiveness and love
Location: Heart, lungs, arms, shoulders, breasts, upper torso

Psychological Issues: Forgiveness, hope, grief, openness to growth and change
Color: Green
Sacrament: Marriage
Sacred Truth: Love is Divine Power

Chakra 3 *Center of Personal Power:* Responsibility and self esteem
Location: Navel region and all organs of the abdomen
Psychological Issues: Trust, fear, self esteem, gut instinct
Color: Yellow
Sacrament: Confirmation
Sacred Truth: Honor Oneself

Chakra 2 *Center of Physical Power:* Safety and sexuality
Location: Sex organs, pelvis, hips, large intestines
Psychological Issues: Sexuality, control, guilt, money, creativity
Color: Orange
Sacrament: Communion
Sacred Truth: Honor One Another

Chakra 1 *Center of Tribal Power:* Safety in the physical world
Location: Base of spine, bones, legs, feet, immune system
Psychological Issues: Physical safety and security, ability to provide for self
Color: Red
Sacrament: Baptism
Sacred Truth: All Is One

*Not recognized widely, information incomplete

ARCHETYPE AND CHAKRA INTEGRATION

I found limited literature which discusses archetype and chakra integration. This concept remains theoretical. So far as I know, no empirical study has been done to support it. However, my intuition tells me that this was the process by which I was healed. This study analyzed my waking dreams to determine if a feasible theoretical explanation for my healing can be found using this concept of archetypal and chakra alignment and integration.

Wauters (1997) maintains that by working with the energy centers of the body, we can have an indication of where they are blocked. By working with the archetypes, we can understand which issues must be dealt with and resolved if we are to evolve to a higher consciousness. Linking chakras and archetypes can directly affect and enhance both the levels of vitality and the issues involving personal power and responsibility with how well we love ourselves and consequently others. The more willing we are to take responsibility and to manage our issues of power, the more evolved the archetype will become, and consequently, the more energetic we will be. As the energy system is cleared of blocks and the archetypes evolve, we can grow and mature into who we are meant to be. Dream work, meditation, body work, homeopathy, prayer, and ritual are a few of the tools that are available to assist with this process. Because archetypes operate on the physical or tribal, psychological or personal, and spiritual or symbolic levels, the chakras can, ideally, channel the energy which is needed for use on each level. The archetypes and the chakras work together synergistically to initiate movement and encourage this evolutionary process which Jung calls the transcendent function. "Connecting the archetypes with the chakras is a relatively new concept which has come out of attempting to unite energy awareness with spiritual growth" (p. 1).

Wauters (1997) continues with the discussion of the integration of archetypes and energy centers:

> This is the working principle by which archetypes and related energy centers, known as chakras, function in the human energy system. Whenever we have problems with a particular issue, such as lack of self-love, this will be reflected in lowered energy in the relevant chakra, and a need to work with the related archetype .... Working with the chakras help us to understand where our energy is blocked, while working with the archetypes shows us which attitudes or emotional issues we need to examine in order to move on to the next, higher stage. (p. 21)

According to Jamal, (1987) the experience of an archetype aligning with an energy center can cause an instantaneous shift in perception and belief which makes it possible to reframe or unlearn limitations and negative perceptions and instantaneously re-program.

Braden (1997) states: "To 'become' requires a shift in viewpoint, changing your body chemistry, by shifting viewpoints, is perhaps the single most powerful tool available to you for the remainder of your life" (p. 182).

The central question this study addresses is whether the healing I experienced can be explained as a process of the archetypal images acting on the chakra system. No empirical evidence can be given to definitively answer this question. Circumstantial or situational evidence, however, suggests this may be so. This evidence is presented in an analysis and discussion of the waking dreams and their effect upon my body, mind, and spirit.

CHAPTER 3

PRESENTATION AND ANALYSIS
OF WAKING DREAMS

BACKGROUND

As noted in Chapter 1, during my seven-year healing journey I logged over 500 waking dreams. They were spontaneous, always very clear, generally brief, sometimes presented as a series over days or intermittently over weeks. One advantage of waking dreams is that I can always recall the experience. I can remember the dream in its entirety years after it occurred.

While most dreams occurred as I practiced my Biogenics pain management program, on occasion they occurred when I was doing something else. One time I had a spontaneous image while I was driving, and I have experienced several while in church. These I called inwardly perceived visions because they have a different texture and feel to them.

SELECTION PROCESS

In reviewing my 500 waking dreams, I discovered recurring themes and images (archetypes) and I started to identify those particular dreams which had the most personal impact on me. Somewhat intuitively, I selected those 41 waking dreams which were most representative of these recurring archetypal images and/or those dreams which had a lasting, profound effect on me. This selection was complete, of course, before beginning any analysis regarding archetypal content or chakra involvement.

PRESENTATION METHOD

The following system is used for the presentation of the waking dreams. First, I identify the date of the waking dreams so their chronology and progression is clear. Second, I describe the waking dream. Third, I discuss the archetypal images, and the impact they had upon me on three levels: physically (tribal) and/or psychologically (personal) and/or spiritually (symbolical). Myss (1996) calls these three levels of power external, internal and symbolic. Fourth, I identify and discuss the chakras affected. I also provide a summary table for each waking dream.

May 10, 1988 — Shealy Clinic

It begins …

We were sent back to our apartments from a long day at the pain clinic with instructions to do our Biogenics homework. On this day, we had practiced biofeedback relaxation techniques while holding a thermometer to see if we could raise the temperature in our hands. I had really liked the two hours that we spent with these exercises, but I had achieved only minimal results.

During the day, we had also had physical therapy, psychological testing, lab work, an exercise period, and a lecture on nutrition. I was tired but optimistic. My intuition told me that I was in the right place; however, I knew that I would have to practice the relaxation exercise religiously. I was becoming increasingly aware that I was "wound very tight" and that the chronic pain was exacerbated by all the tension that I had always carried in my musculature.

Myss stated in Shealy (1999) that healing, by definition, is a sacred art (p. vii). Prayer, our connection to the sacred, has long been held by most religious traditions to contain great healing power. My faith tradition teaches that prayers, visions, and dreams touch the heart and spirit of us all, regardless of physical time and distance.

I have always believed in healing prayer, and so after a light evening meal, I said a simple prayer asking for protection and healing. This is still my practice. I settled in with my tape recorder and homework tape and began to follow the instructions.

"My feet are heavy and warm. My legs are heavy and warm. My thighs are heavy and warm." I repeated each phrase three times.

Just then, I "saw" a clear, bright image of my little girl. Although I recognized her immediately, I was very surprised because she was so very happy. With arms over her head, she jumped up and down. Her dark Dutch Boy bob flew away from her face and her large blue eyes sparkled with sheer delight! She looked in my eyes and I felt "realer than real" as I connected with her in a way that I felt what she felt: I was intensely alive; intensely happy; intensely whole and intensely aware that I would never be the same. She seemed to be saying "Well, finally ...."

According to Jung (1958), the child archetype is generally believed to carry the birthing of a new consciousness — certainly a new awareness breaking into consciousness. Innocent and vulnerable, this archetype has great transforming power. The appearance of a happy child in dreams is associated with inner creativity and spontaneity and is indicative of a spiritual change. The child has a free connection to the inner world with all of its imagination, spontaneity, and creativity. The child is potential future and paves the way for a future change of personality. In the individuation process, it anticipates the figure that comes from the synthesis of conscious and unconscious elements in the personality. It is therefore a unifying symbol which unites the opposites, and brings about wholeness.

As a child, I had almost always been sad. I remember few carefree, joyful times in childhood. I was often tense, always expecting the worst. It was my perception that I was to carry the emotional dysfunction of my whole family of birth (total of seven). I was an emotional victim. Because the victim archetype is at the lowest levels of energy and awareness, it is stuck at the tribal level, frozen in fear or terror. My perception was that I had no personal power. My tribe held power over me.

As Bruyere (1989) points out, "While anger, fear and pain are in themselves natural ways for the body to protect itself, misdirected or suppressed anger, repressed or excessive fear and chronic pain are all indications of imbalance in the first chakra" (p. 199). I find it interesting that much of my chronic pain was in my low back, hip and knees.

This incredible image was a beginning of promise and healing for me. I understand now why this one image was so powerful. When the archetype of my happy little girl appeared and changed my attitude (about myself) or belief or perspective (from sad to happy), energy shifted from the negative to positive; to a lighter, freer level with its freedom of expression, joy and ease. Negative energy (sadness) was transformed into a positive energy (the "knowing" that the healthy, happy little girl is a part of me and is willing and able to help me heal). By healing the outgrown negative perception with its negative energetic state, my archetype could evolve and I could become unstuck and evolve into who I was meant to be. I was free to connect with the universal forces that move through me, bringing much desired creativity, gratitude, and unity. I *felt* the shift from negative to positive energy in my body (mostly below the waist, but also at the heart chakra). In fact, I felt this archetypal image in my musculature.

Sources for dream analysis that follows in this section include Bruyere (1989), Myss (1996), Wauters (1997), Shealy and Myss (1995), and Gerber (2000).

Summary of Waking Dream 1

Archetype: Little Girl acting on the Physical Level and aligning with:

First Chakra: It encouraged the reframing of "childish" perceptions and family or social beliefs that no longer served, letting go of negative family (especially childhood) experiences.

Second Chakra: I tried to control others and find a place for myself by taking on the emotional craziness of my tribe. The resulting depression was habitual and long term.

Third Chakra: I had few boundaries, especially healthy emotional ones. My intuition or *knowings* were discounted by the tribe because they were contrary to the way they wanted to operate. I learned to distrust intuition. Since I seemed different, I thought different meant flawed.

May 19, 1988

I am entering a dark place with my little girl. She says that we need light. I can see outlines of tall, cone shaped objects. I assume that they are trees, but I have never seen such tall, cone-like trees before (spiral shapes). As I ponder just where we are and try to rationally understand the environment, my little girl goes from tree to tree, pressing light switches that are hidden from my view. Each tree comes alive with wonderful white light.

"Why stumble around in the dark?" she asks with a light hearted giggle. As my eyes adjust, I can see My Path clearly for the first time.

Spiral shapes are archetypal; they symbolize cosmic energy and growth. In ancient times the spiral symbolized the breath and the spirit. The Egyptian god Toth is represented with a large spiral on his head which was thought to give him power. It is also noted that the spiral is associated with primitive dances of healing and incantation (Cirlot, 1971).

Trees are considered to be "medicine people of the plant world" by some indigenous cultures and in many cultures they symbolize the process of transformation. The roots are associated with the past and how we honor our heritage and ancestors. Trunks symbolize present life and reveal where the life force and creative spirit are either engaged or not. Branches symbolize desired future goals, or if it is a flowering or fruit tree, the attainment of these goals (Arrien, 1993).

The forest sometimes symbolizes the unconscious, and while forest symbolism is complex, it is connected at all levels with the symbolism of the female principle or of the Great Mother. Jung maintains that the sylvan terrors that figure so prominently in children's tales symbolize the perilous aspects of the unconscious (Cirlot, 1971).

Matthew Fox (1988) believes that mystics are adults who welcome the child within them and Mechtilde of Magdeburg writes in Fox (1988), "God leads the child God has called in wonderful ways. God takes the soul to a secret place, for God alone will play with it in a game of which the body knows nothing. God says, 'I am your playmate! Your childhood was a companion of my Holy Spirit" (p. 195). And so my happy spontaneous, delightful inner child is leading me into myself in a new way, in a new place where we meet cosmic, feminine energy and where the life force and creative spirit can be engaged.

Often I am hesitant to act until I have things figured out logically. I am caught on the hook of my past experiences where I was not allowed to explore and learned to be very cautious of unusual and strange things. It is not surprising that the power source that could transform was hidden from me. I didn't even know where the switches were!

As the little girl stepped confidently to each tree, she was giving me an invaluable gift that I had lost, the gift of childlike wonder and the confidence to risk. As the wonderful light comes on she stands there as though saying, "See what *I've* done." She could rejoice in her accomplishment and appreciate my astonishment without ridiculing me for my inability to know it all.

Again, my perception of having the sad, silent little girl (victim) was reframed and I again felt a shift in my lower energy centers; an easier, freer spontaneity. I also believe that the negative energy of not knowing all that I am was positively affected by the archetypal actions. New personal power energy and better self-esteem result in a healthier, more creative human being — child or not.

One very clear energy shift came from being an intelligent observer to being caught up in delight as the lights came on. "Why stumble around in the dark?" Why, indeed! I can now see My Path.

Summary of Waking Dream 2

Archetype: My Little Girl acting on the Physical Level and aligning with:

First Chakra: Tribal Power is all about us, not me; about conformity, not personal creativity. Having my healthy child as teacher helps me to continue the *me* process in a healthy way.

Second Chakra: Exploration and experimentation without having the tribe dictate the process is self-building.

Third Chakra: Finding the power switches and being able to switch on creativity and the confidence that comes with competency are very healing experiences.

This is a grounding experience. These three chakras are those that channel the earth's energy up to our higher chakras, and in addition, help ground our higher, lighter energies on the material plane. Through these chakras we can manifest our creativity in a physical form. Getting out of our heads into our bodies is a positive result of being grounded. The little girl helps recapture that spontaneous, earthy, natural feeling.

July 15, 1988

"Stay relaxed. Be at ease."

A small ball of light (heat) comes from above and enters my right hand. I feel warmth and energy spread up through my body. Although this is an unusual thing to happen to me, I am not at all uneasy. I can trust this process because it feels authentic, and I know intuitively that it is healing.

July 16, 1988

"Be at ease."

I feel "adjustments" to my back and neck. A warm current

passes through my arms into my shoulders and neck. These are internal adjustments or movements of energy.

I am not sure of the origin of this voice, but because I always entered my healing time as a holy time, always with an attitude of prayer, I believe that I was hearing the voice of the Holy Spirit. However, Wisdom or Sophia may have been speaking. Perhaps it was all of them. Virtually any archetype may bring the transcendent message. I only know that the voice was clear and loving, yet also direct. I will never forget any of the messages it spoke to me.

"Be at ease" was the perfect message. I had never been "at ease." I could not relax, even to go to sleep. This directive was more effective than the "Stay relaxed" because it spoke of safety, security, trust, and acceptance. Overall, the feeling was one of having a loving parent draw me close and tell me a wonderful story. In a way, I was being re-parented.

I had several images with energy being activated and moved in and around my body. This movement was largely due to the relaxation and reprogramming exercises, I thought. I had not heard of the energy centers at this time.

Summary of Waking Dream 3 (both dreams above)

Archetype: Wisdom (Holy Spirit) acting on the Physical Level and aligning with:

First Chakra: This image continued the process of positive reframing of tribal perspectives. It promoted a sense of security and safety which released negative energy in my first chakra.

Third Chakra: As I trust this healing process, I gain confidence in my own healing potential and my self-esteem is strengthened, my personal power is enhanced, the third chakra is cleared of negative energy and pain is relieved.

July 17, 1988

"Stay relaxed. You are called."

"What is it that I am to do?"

"Only that for which you have been prepared for since the beginning."

I see a configuration of what I understand is a spirit. I experience a lot of warmth and small energy charges, especially in legs and lower back.

I had been rather obsessive at this time about what I was going to do; the position at the college where I had been for 18 years no longer seemed a good choice. A new division chairperson seemed to be very doubtful that we could work together, and she made that very obvious.

I had been responsible for creating and operating a Center for Independent Study (CIS) to accommodate the diverse needs of an extremely diverse student body, mostly older and under-prepared students who needed alternatives to the traditional academic structures. The CIS was a success on main campus and in several satellite locations. It was time to leave.

So, I asked often and lengthily, "What am I going to do? What is my purpose now? What does God want me to do?"

Myss (1995) points out that these are not ordinary questions; they are depth charges that unlock the rumblings of the soul. They certainly were for me. Most of us at various crisis points and transitions have these kinds of questions. We need a purpose regardless of age.

In contrast, when a woman of the Dagara tribe in the West Africa nation of Burkina Faso becomes pregnant, elders put her into a hypnotic trance and invite the unborn child to reveal its mission in life. The response is channeled through the mother, who speaks in a child's thin voice. This way, the child will not have to fight to remember the purpose of his or her life. The

Dagara believe that children arrive carrying information from the other world. During this ritual, the elders can ask what they can do to make the way safe, to help avoid wounding the child (Somé, 1994).

Shealy and Myss (1995) believe that each individual makes a sacred contract prior to birth that becomes the driving motivation throughout life. Each soul agrees to encounter a cluster of archetypes in an educational relationship. Each contract is very individual but has in common with all others the wise use of responsible, loving power.

I did not know about any of this when I was asking my question 12 years ago, but looking back, my purpose was being gifted to me as I learned to heal. This image is one of several that dealt with this theme: "Only that for which you have been prepared for since the beginning." This became a new focus for me and what a comfort. I began to relax and realize that God's will for me *was* unfolding, and I *could* trust the process. I was content to live my questions. It was enough.

I experienced "energy zips" in the first and second chakras where most of the pain was centered. While I knew little about energy systems and archetypes at the time, I felt exhilarated and excited. What a change!

Summary of Waking Dream 4

Archetype: Wisdom (Holy Spirit) acting on the Physical and Spiritual Levels and aligning with:

First Chakra: Physical Power

Fifth Chakra: Will Power

July 18, 1988

I see an image of four doors opening into each other. I am feeling light and well so I open them one by one. A voice speaks.

"You will heal as you are healed."

"You will teach as you are taught."

"You will comfort as you are comforted."

"You will counsel as you are counseled."

This is a companion image, or follow-up, after the one on July 17, 1988. It gave me the specifics of my calling.

Something about this image infused me with energy from the very beginning. I was feeling light and well as I opened the doors. Ordinarily, I would be cautious about opening closed doors.

I am reminded here of the admonition of some wise person: "Let your mission find you."

"You will heal (make or become well) *as you are healed."* I had never thought of myself as a healer, a wounded one at that. But then I had never before been healed on all levels from the inside out.

"You will teach (instruct, provide with knowledge or insight) *as you are taught."* I was trained as a teacher, but college was nowhere near as exciting as this experience! Was I going to teach the healing techniques I had learned in the School of Pain?

"You will comfort (soothe in distress or sorrow, console, be with accurate empathy) *as you are comforted."* I now know how to comfort those in pain.

"You will counsel (give advice, mutual exchange of ideas, plan, recommend) *as you are counseled."* I was finishing a Master's degree in counseling at this time, but I learned *much* more from the images.

It seems to me that these four are much the same if treating the whole person is the goal. Good healers teach, counsel, comfort. Good teachers heal, counsel, comfort.

I was still somewhat uneasy about what I was going to do, but after this image (and the previous image on July 17th) I relaxed and let it all unfold. This was another pivotal image because it did give me focus. The more I thought about the message, the more it seemed a true assessment of what I had wanted to do with my life, but I had never dreamed that I could do it all.

Summary of Waking Dream 5

Archetype: Wisdom (Holy Spirit) acting on the Physical and Psychological Levels and aligning with:

First, Second, and Third Chakras: I was being introduced to myself, and I was having some realizations of just who I was apart from tribal conditioning and expectations which had directed me: "Go to college and get a teaching degree so you will have insurance in case something happens. Then, get married and have children." I was becoming more willing to give up control and to trust. I was experiencing a period of great creativity, and I had never thought that I was creative. I was experiencing a healthier self-esteem than I had ever had. Consequently, I was healing physically, psychologically, and spiritually. I could feel it all happen.

Sixth Chakra: Here is the link between mental body, intelligence, and physiological characteristics. The Sacrament of Ordination is this center's symbolic sacrament. It represents the task one is called to do in service to others (Myss 1996).

September 18, 1988

I come upon three Wise Ones who are fashioning figures out of earth (clay). Each spoke in turn.

"I am fashioning form out of formlessness."

"I am fashioning time out of timelessness."
"I am fashioning space out of infinity."
"Contemplate!"

"In the beginning was the Word (Logos) and Word was with God and the Word was God" (John 1:1, The Open Bible New American Standard).

Brown (1982) writes that in several cultures words have special potency or force: What is named is really present. Words and their sounds are born in the breath of the one from whom they proceed. Words are sacred and must be used with care and responsibility. However, words are also very limiting; they cannot convey the depth and nuance of what they describe. Recitation of a myth of creation, for example, is understood to be an actual, not symbolic, retelling of that primitive creative process, which is outside the bounds of time.

It is most amazing to experience creation spirituality; to come upon three (the number of spiritual synthesis) Wise Ones who are in the process of forming representations of beings out of clay (primal matter). Their words were amplified, their meaning extended:

"I am giving particular shape to amorphous shapelessness."

"I am marking set periods out of eternity, which is not affected by time."

"I am molding boundless expanse, extending in all directions, out of unlimited, endless, immeasurable space or time."

They created in a framework of matter, time, and space. The experience of time and space appear to be familiar concepts to native people. They think in terms of the circle, cyclical and reciprocal. Time is cyclical, not linear; time, space, and matter are anchored around the creative, mystic center.

In diagrams of the cosmos, the central space is always

reserved for the Creator who appears as if surrounded by a circular shaped halo (formed by the intersection of the circle of heaven and the circle of the earth) surrounded by concentric circles extending outwards, and by the wheel of the Zodiac. In Western emblems, an eagle's head sometimes carries the significance of this infinite being (Cirlot, 1971).

I am told to "Contemplate," that is, "to observe; to gaze at intently; to study or expect or intend; to meditate or muse" (Crowther, et. al, 1995). I actually think that the message is to stay awake and pay attention; to focus on the creative process at every level from atom to cosmos and to appreciate the wonders of the gifts of intuition and imagination. Contemplation requires a willingness to be transformed, and I feel that I *am* being re-created, and that I *am* in the hands of those sacred Wise Ones. They are demonstrating in a very creative, yet practical way what I am a witness to, and I am co-creator of this dynamic life process called wholeness.

Jones (1992) writes that contemplation becomes an integral, vital part of journeying, of pilgrimage. It requires a vital concentration and discipline as the way becomes more wonderful and unfamiliar.

I find it very meaningful that many artists perceive arts and crafts as sacred creations. Native peoples believe that all of life is sacred, and they have no separate words for arts or crafts. Instead, all of life is an experience of creation (Walters, 1989).

Summary of Waking Dream 6
Archetype: Wise Ones acting on the Physical, Psychological and Spiritual (Creation) levels and aligning with:

First Chakra: The Sacred Truth, All is One, is particularly relevant here. I appreciate how this image made me feel more grounded and that it gave me a visceral appreciation for the sacred acts of creation.

Fourth Chakra: This center mediates between body and spirit and determines their power. I feel that particular synergy between body, mind, and spirit that results when all working together create more than each can alone. Entering into our own hearts, the tribal heart is left behind. Working on personal wounds, we learn to heal self by releasing and letting go to the Divine Will and by realizing that everything in and about our life runs off the fuel of the heart and that the only path toward spiritual consciousness is through the heart (Myss, 1996).

Sixth Chakra: This center is tied to the energies of the psyche, both conscious and unconscious psychological forces. Insight, intuition, and wisdom are activated here. I believe this center is activated by this image. (Not only when I first experienced it but any time I remember it.) It is like having a pump primed, intuitively speaking. Wisdom is light in the psychological sense, and this chakra activates lessons that lead to wisdom.

September 27, 1988

As I walk on my path, houses with all sorts of strange shapes spring up.

Some are triangles.

Some are circles.

Some are rectangles.

Some are shaped like question marks.

The people who come out of the houses are shaped like their houses.

"We become what we conform to."

Tribal power is all about conformity. The emphasis at this level of experience is on loyalty and identification. We can, through tribal power, become what we conform to, which can serve us or not.

This image reminds me in an interesting and engaging way that I can, and must, outgrow family belief systems that no longer serve in a positive way; I can and must let go of negative perceptions about my tribe. It is disconcerting to realize that although I no longer believe some negative perceptions, they can still have power over me.

Maintaining a healthy sense of pride in ancestry and family traditions is important, and native families can give love and support. Each person, however, must build a unique house and grow out of trying to control the size and shape of other "houses." Leaving the tribe and taking full responsibility for all of life's challenges and gifts is a way of building a strong house, one that conforms but leaves room for transformation.

I must become aware of my negative perceptions remaining from my tribe and unplug my energy from them. Since so much of my chronic pain was in the tribal energy center, I realized that I still had much work. Two of the negative beliefs that still had power over me were, "Thinking people are superior to feeling people," and "The scientist is more valuable than the poet." It was not long after this image that the Wise Ones helped me build my own spiritual house.

Summary of Waking Dream 7

Archetype: Wisdom or Wise Ones acting on the Physical Level and aligning with:

First Chakra: There is a kind of smothering security to negative tribal beliefs. Outgrowing them is the challenge here.

Second Chakra: Creativity cannot flow unless it is from

the place of personal creativity.

Third Chakra: A necessary part of the journey is learning to trust one's inner wisdom and learning to unplug from criticism that can stunt creativity and selfhood.

December 16, 1988

The Great Wise One and I are on a ledge above the valley. He is playing some kind of flute. As he plays, people appear out of the instrument. He is calling out the Ancestors of the Ages. When six are around me, they begin a circular dance with me in the center. As the Wisest One continues to play, the ancestors tell me that they are giving me wisdom: "Fore-seeing" "Re-membering" "Re-collecting" "Mind-ing" "Be-lieving" "Form-ing"

Arrien (1993) speaks of ancestral influence. She points out that there are cultures that believe ancestor spirits literally stand behind us to support us in our life, dreams, and purpose and are invested in seeing present generations and future generations fulfill their dreams and purposes. She states that some cultures believe that ancestor spirits can help us through the last doorway in the process we call dying.

Arrien (1993) quotes from Milton's *Paradise Lost* to suggest the unlimited resources of our heritage and lineage that is honored through ancestor spirits. "Millions of spiritual creatures walk the Earth / unseen, both when we wake and when we sleep …." Arrien continues: "Many shamanic traditions classify Milton's spiritual creatures as ancestors who are biological family, extended family, friends, and figures in history who give inspiration" (p. 116).

In this image we are off my path, on a ledge above a valley which indicates a spiritual perspective. The Great Wise One is playing a flute whose sound is related to inner feminine intuitive feeling. He calls out six highly evolved ancestors. Six comprises the union of the two triangles (of fire and water) and hence signifies the human soul. The ancestors form a circle (symbol of eternity, completeness, perfection). Jung's psychological implication includes the notion that the circle corresponds to the ultimate state of oneness. They place me in the center and they dance, that is, they move physically around me, which generates certain rhythmic vibrations. The dance is considered one of the most ancient forms of magic and there is universal belief that it is a symbol of the act of creation and is the incarnation of eternal energy (Cirlot, 1971).

Brooke Medicine Eagle, in *Healers on Healing* (Carlson and Shield, 1989) writes this description of a Native American healing circle:

A circle would be called together in which the diseased one would be laid in the center. The circle might begin by cleansing itself of past history through acts of personal forgiveness; then, the singers might sing songs of harmony. They would dance an imagined ascending spiral, calling and drawing the descending energy of the one in the center, until the descent hesitates, stops and begins to lift upward, carried by the community energy but gradually gaining its own energy. At last, it would resonate fully within the newly healed one as he or she rejoins the dance. (p. 60)

As the ancestors dance, they impart wisdom that usually is not available to us in our human form. This seems to me to be a kind of physical intercessory prayer as well as wisdom. This wisdom involves:

Fore-seeing — to predict or understand *before*, to prophecy *before;* the four ways of seeing: intuition, insight, perception and vision.

Prefix 're' meaning 'back again or anew' (Crowther et all 1995).

Re-membering — bringing to mind *in new ways;* call back to mind (Crowther, et all, 1995). To remember is to "call to heart" according to Grassi (1987).

Re-collecting — to gather again; to remember again (Crowther, et all, 1995). In Kavanaugh & Rodreguiz (trans. 1979), Teresa of Avila used this term to mean "drawing near to God because the soul collects its faculties together and enters into itself to be with God."

Mind-ing — memory; opinion; have in mind; to intend; being in the present in a *new way* (Crowther, et all, 1995).

Believe-ing — to feel sure of truth; existence. Being open to old truths on new levels (Crowther, et all, 1995).

Form-ing — to shape; to mold; to train or instruct; to give character to; spiritual creativity (Crowther, et all, 1995).

I am given the gifts (wisdom) of prophecy, of remembering in new ways, of drawing near again, of being in the present in a new way, of being open to old truths on new levels and of shaping or molding with a new kind of creativity. The Wise Ones are bearers of the light of consciousness because wisdom is one kind of light.

Summary of Waking Dream 8

Archetype: The Great Wise One acting on the Spiritual Level and aligning with:

First Chakra: Although we never really lose our embeddedness in our biological family we can reframe and change perspectives of tribal conditioning and raise our consciousness of what is possible. This center is also about being grounded in the life force and about honor codes that make us honorable human beings. Strengthening the tribal characteristics of being open to the wisdom of the ancestors is an issue here.

Second Chakra: The creative energy available in the second chakra helps us to break out of habitual patterns of thoughts, behaviors and relationships that do not serve us. Creative energy here helps to re-shape our lives, bodies and spirits. Positive ancestor energy can help us to re-collect and re-member.

Third Chakra: Energy here can help re-order our lives and evaluate our relationship to power. At issue here is the choice of choosing spirit over illusions of physical circumstances. The stronger the energy here, the fewer connections to negative people and experiences. Positive tribal spirituality is about the healthy honoring of ancestors, honoring life giving rituals, and expanding awareness of what creativity really is.

January 9, 1989

I am kneeling by an alter crying. A Wise One appears and gestures for me to rise. "The wounded healer heals best. Go heal!"

Jones (1992) has stated that the "wounded healer carries within him a wound and a gift: the wound of love and the gift of love" (p. 20). Achterberg (1985) writes that the concept of the wounded healer is common, but is often associated with the shaman. The calling of the native shaman (includes many kinds of healers) often involves surviving an acute physical, spiritual, or mental crisis. Joan Halifax writes that this wounding (or initiation) often comes as a crisis or powerful illness involving an encounter with forces of decay and destruction. The wounded healer acquires wisdom through the wounding and resulting transformation. "Illness thus becomes the vehicle to a higher plane of consciousness" (p. 21).

Wounded healers need to be aware that they can slip into the shadow, the victim, the martyr, or the rescuer archetype. I certainly felt like a victim on many levels and many times during my illnesses. One of the best ways to break out of the victim archetype is to do something positive. Since I never thought of myself as a healer, this was a positive message, a lifting up and a sending forth with a divine mission. I felt this resonate in my belly and in my soul. Historically, religion and healing have always been connected. In a sense, as Shealy (1999) points out, all healing is sacred and all therapies intended for healing are sacred. (I find it interesting that just one month after I had this image, the Shaman archetype appeared.)

Summary of Waking Dream 9

Archetype: Wise One, Wounded Healer (Calling of) acting on the Physical and Psychological Levels and aligning with:

First Chakra: Reframing a sense of self in relation to the tribe and the sacred helps me to move away from negative tribal identification and helps me to identify and appreciate the sacred in my life.

Third Chakra: I move out of the largely unconscious role of the victim as my self esteem is strengthened.

Fourth Chakra: Reframing victim consciousness raises hope, and the role of wounded healer makes me committed to helping others. I can be compassionate because I have received compassion and I am free to explore the healing gifts of forgiveness and love.

January 24, 1989

The Great Wise One and I are kneeling in my path. We are creating a sand painting. We trace red sand on the spine, hips, legs, and lower back. We trace the shoulders and neck and arms with bright green sand. The Great Wise One surrounds the figure with gold, and a few inches away from the body, he adds a rainbow which outlines the body. (The figure is mine, and this ritual is helping me heal.)

According to Achterberg (1985) sand paintings are central elements in Navajo healing. They represent the spiritual and physical landscape in which the patient and illness exist, the etiology of the disease and the mythology chosen for cure. The patient is drawn into a symbolic drama which combines visualization, chanting, drumming, and divination which is the corollary to western medicine's diagnostic procedures.

A beautiful and powerful ceremony, sand painting is meant to restore harmony and wholeness and to bring the person into a renewed sense of and connection with Spirit/life. The primary emphasis is on the restoration or establishment of inner harmony. The belief is that health returns when harmony is restored. Sand paintings are created between sunrise and sunset of the same day and are destroyed at the end of that day (Achterberg, 1985).

I realize, looking back, how much I needed grounding if I were to heal. If grounding is not stable, the spirit breaks down. It cannot carry the lower chakra's negative weight. This image is an effort to achieve that healthy grounding. In its great and simple beauty and creativity, there are rich symbolic elements: the outline of the body which is drawn with tender care and beauty; my involvement with the process in a very meaningful way; the sacred intent and creative method in which I was being prayed into wholeness.

Red sand traces the tribal chakras where I had so much pain, both physical and psychic. The green sand traces the fourth chakra center of emotional power with its issues of grief (so much unmourned loss), forgiveness (perceived unhealed hurts), resentment (against perceived insults at work), and unresolved issues of commitment (what was I to do now).

As Myss (1995) pointed out much later in the workshops and in her writing, energy was being drained by negative beliefs, perceptions, and attitudes. She emphasized the need to unplug from the negative and draw back my energy so that I could heal. Images such as this helped.

Gold is a synonym for light in some languages, so the Wisest One surrounds my body with light, repairing the aura and bringing the energy (light) back into my body. The rainbow is a beautiful finishing touch, a covenant of loving protection. I felt truly cared for.

Summary of Waking Dream 10

Archetype: Wisest One acting on the Physical and Psychological Levels and aligning with:

First Chakra: The Wise One used primal elements of nature and their symbolism to heal.

Second Chakra: Issues here included control by others and unused creativity. I was surprised at how positive I felt about this creative ritual. My body, mind, and spirit responded beautifully.

Fourth Chakra: Family forgiveness issues needed healing; grief over loss of physical health and resentment over perceived negative treatment at my work. These were ongoing issues on several levels that required changing and maintaining shifts in perception.

January 29, 1989

A different Wise One is standing in a clearing near my path. He seems to be playing some game with some objects. As I watch, I realize that he picks the objects out of the air.

He hits two clouds together like cymbals to get attention. He picks two bolts of lightening out of the air and makes thunder. He jumps up and down on a cloud and makes thunder. He motions with his hands and rain, then snow, then hail falls from his fingers.

He catches a ray of sun and focuses it on the ground along my path.

"Power is the issue! Connect-Create-Transform!"

"The common ingredient in every single energy dysfunction is an issue of power" (Myss, 1995). "Each Sacred Contract is individual, but one thing they have in common is to learn the wise, responsible, loving use of power" (Shealy, 1995).

Power *is* the issue. Using power to connect, create, and transform is a powerful message. This image echoes throughout my body, mind, and spirit yet today, years after the experience. When I think of it, I experience inner resonance, and I know that this subtle power is still operating on many levels.

As I reflect, I am reminded of the ancient God Zeus, who was a consort to the powerful nature goddesses. He used the elements as weapons or as evidence of his power: He slew with lightening and hammered his enemies with thunder. Zeus was the sky and weather god of antiquity. He was called the "cloud gatherer," but he was also the all powerful, the protector, and ruler of the family of man (Stapleton, 1986).

DeQuincy (2000) observes that people lose power or fail to utilize available power because they are literally out of touch with the power of nature and the elements. They no longer participate in nature's cycle of creation and annihilation.

Instead they protect themselves from inevitable dangers in nature, becoming isolated from its animate and inanimate healing process. No longer do they hear the Earth's voices, no longer respond to her calling or participate in her carnal exchange. The loss is mutual and profound.

Another very different kind of power can be inferred here. This is the power of alchemy. The alchemist archetype exhibits a magical or mysterious power or process of transforming one thing into another. Metaphysically, the alchemist transmutes lead into gold, using a combination of chemistry, magic, and philosophy that deals with the mystery of matter and the creation of life. This transmuter's spiritual goal is to harmonize the human individual with the universe (Shealy, 1995).

Edinger (1979) asserts that on the psychological and spiritual levels the redemption by God was a theme basic to alchemy: The alchemical opus was a work of redemption. Psychological development in all of its phases is a redemption process. It is a power process and a creative process, and it cannot occur without intentional connectedness.

According to some, there is a belief that the alchemists were simply failed chemists; however, their attempts to change lead into gold were not their primary purpose. The alchemical process encoded key stages of psychological growth and development. Alchemists believed that psychological and spiritual development were very closely parallel and the final alchemical stage, symbolized by gold, sun, and royalty, signifies the successful ability to manifest a spiritual truth on a physical level (Pearson, 1991).

This image and its power message operated on many levels. Certainly, it was very powerful on the physical or grounding level. Wauters (1997) emphasizes that the grounding that we all need to be healthy is available as a result of the connection to and between all living organisms. Without grounding, or getting out of the head into the body, the connections with higher, lighter energies will be uncertain. Sometimes, it may be impossible to sustain them. Only by maintaining a direct and conscious link with the physical body can the accumulated emotional energy of daily life be discharged. Negative archetypes may appear when grounding is neglected or lost.

Interestingly, the seven chakras of the human body bear the same relationship to each other as the Solar System planets have to each other. This solar energy is received into the body through the chakras; each energy center receives a particular solar energy. By remaining in touch with all of nature we can receive this primal power that can help keep us healthy and in balance.

Energetic abilities and power to create lead to energetic abilities to transform consciousness: body, mind, spirit, family, community, organizations, and the environment. Everything *is* connected in a spiral of power.

Summary of Waking Dream 11

Archetypes: The Wise One (Alchemist) acting on the Physical and Psychological Levels and aligning with:

First Chakra: I am reminded that I neglect my connection to nature and the elements that I experienced when I was a barefooted kid. I need this kind of power (grounding) as a strong foundation for the higher energies.

Second Chakra: I realize that I need to reconnect with others and support others so that our sources of power, both internal and external, can be used in positive, cooperative ways. Creative energy, if allowed to flow, will continuously act to reshape individual lives and reveal meaning to events.

Fifth Chakra: Surrendering personal will to Divine Will,

will help with my own transformation on every level, and I will have the energy to help others transform themselves, organizations, and society.

When an archetype aligns with an energy center as happens in this experience, a shift in perception can occur very rapidly, very completely. The power that is available then is the issue: connecting, creating, and transforming on every level in a responsible, wise, loving way.

Rays of sun focused on my path may be a promise of continual illumination; of walking in the light; of guidance along my path; of the power to "see" all of my responsibilities and all of my blessings.

February 2, 1989

A Wise One beckons me off my path. He tells me that he and his friends are helping to build my spiritual house. He says that I may come in the house but that it is not quite finished.

I enter through a door marked Wisdom under an arch called Protection. The floors are Faith covered with Humility. The walls are Pure Intuition covered with Discernment. The roof is woven of Love and Integrity.

A large plant grows in the middle of the room. Three large white roses are in bloom. They are Fulfillment, Health, and Hope.

There is a balcony all around called Vision and Insight.

"For every house is built by someone; but the builder of all things is God." Hebrews 3:4 (The Open Bible New American Standard).

"What is a home but a merging of our lost selves? What is a home but our divided selves finally embracing" (Wiederkehr, 1988, p. 13).

Spinoza has stated that spiritual intuition is knowledge of God; that spiritual intuition is associated with mystical experience and at this level is "pure." This kind of intuition brings into being new, fresh, creative possibilities. It certainly brings into question perceptions regarding our beliefs, maybe the whole belief system that runs our lives. The process is one of exploring, questioning, and perhaps, almost invariably, changing some of the assumptions and perceptions long held and which no longer serve (Vaughan, 1979).

This image is, I believe, a classic work of the Holy Spirit, and I believe that this building of my spiritual house was crucial and timely to my healing. There is no true, physical healing without the influence and leadership of one's spirit, under the influence of the Spirit.

The symbols in this image are rich with meaning. Mystics have always considered the feminine aspect of the universe as a chest, a house, or an outdoor garden. Another symbolic association is that which equates the house with the repository of all wisdom, that is, tradition itself. In dreams, the house may represent the different layers of the psyche (Cirlot, 1971).

The rose has been a powerful religious and mythic symbol through the ages. It symbolizes perfection, eternity, fertility, passion, and mystery of life. The white rose is sometimes called the "flower of light" because of its connotation of spiritual unfolding. Robert Assagioli has been known to use the image of the white rose to help explain the unfolding process of the psyche. Aromatherapists know that the rose scent induces relaxation and dispels depression, anxiety and grief (Campbell 1994).

The path of transformation leads from a life of requirements and measuring up (to God or culture) to a life of relationship with God. From anxiety to trust and a life centered in the Divine (Borg, 1995). This is a belief that engages my heart and soul. As Jones (1985) proclaims, "The ordinary, simplistic, bland pablum of popular religion simply will not do anymore." He then asks the question, "How can I be a believer in today's world in such a way that it involves my whole self-my passion, my intelligence and my allegiance" (p. 20)? I would add "and my imagination."

Our tribal beliefs must be examined. Tribal rules and tribal spirituality sometimes do not fit. We must build and dwell in our own spiritual house. I had never thought of imagining an actual spiritual house or a house for my spirit; in fact, I suppose that I unconsciously thought of the church structure as a spiritual house for all people. Having these images where the Wise Ones carry out the directive to build one especially for me has been so fantastic. It seems to be one of those sixth chakra extravagant possibilities that Myss (1996) talks about.

My roots are Southern Baptist; my perception of my early, tribal conditioning is rife with judgment and guilt. I was a sponge for all of the negative theology and little of the positive. I was never at home in this milieu, but I did not know where home was.

For 40 years, I have been a United Methodist, active in directing choirs, teaching, and intercessory prayer ministry. This fit better while I was extraverting my spirituality. For the past ten years, with this intense healing process, my spirituality has taken another shape and another direction. I am more introverted, more prayerful, more compassionate, less judging, and I desire the fruits of a closer, deeper relationship with the Divine. The Holy Spirit, the master builder of spiritual houses, is very much a companion now and is, I believe, the mediator between my conscious and my unconscious mind.

From the viewpoint of energetic healing, unless the spiritual centers are sanctified and consecrated, they are not powerful enough to aid in the transcendence of the lower chakras. As the spiritual chakras assist in the evolution, more energy is available to reframe negative perceptions that drain power and make us vulnerable to dis-ease. Thus the whole energy system becomes more aware, more resilient, more powerful (Wauters, 1997).

The highest function of each chakra is expressed in a sacred truth that points the way to physical health *and* spiritual integration. It is also true that all archetypes evolve, eventually, into spirituality (Myss, 1996).

Summary of Waking Dream 12

Archetypes: Wise Ones (Holy Spirit) and Spiritual House acting on the Spiritual Level and aligning with:

First Chakra: Reframing of tribal spirituality is a necessary part of the individual spiritual journey. The faith of my father and mother may not be specific enough for me.

Third Chakra: I feel comfortable surrounded by intuition (internal understanding; guide) and know that I must temper intuition with discrimination (discernment).

Fourth Chakra: I walk on a foundation of confidence (faith) which must be covered with humility (obedience) if I am to serve self, others, and God. My roof (covering) is compassion (love) for all and honor (integrity) toward all. This is possible only through the divine power of love.

Sixth Chakra: The Holy Spirit, or Sophia, the Magna Mater, welcomes me and I am under the protection (safety, security) of the Wise Ones.

February 10, 1989

The Shaman Appears.

I am on my path. I become so tired I lie down. It is sunny and warm so I fall asleep. As I sleep, part of me sees a body rising out of my body — a slender, short male who looks primitive. He has a wall-eye and he carries a stick with a gourd rattle and a few feathers attached. He goes about shaking the rattle around and under plants, rocks, and trees.

While a part of me watches in amazement, he goes into my spiritual house and hunts around — all the time using the rattle and humming a rather atonal song. Finally, he comes to my large plant. The rattle changes, telling him that what he is seeking is in the earth around the plant. He digs out what looks like a coin made of stone or bone and places it on my alter.

Then, he comes back to my body and rejoins me. I awaken, go to my house and find the coin. It is apparently rare and only for me.

"Shamans have long understood that we need go nowhere but inside ourselves for our transformation" (Doore, 1988, p. 210).

In Mayan culture, persons with eyes that deviated from the normal, were said to have the duty and the privilege of looking into the future (Sams and Carson, 1988).

Doore (1988) indicates that shamanism seems to capture the attention of an increasing number of people possibly because it is a response to a situation that many regard as a severe crisis. Reasons for this may be found in the earthiness and groundedness of shamanism, as well as the fact that shamanic work seems to further the balance between humans and nature, thus appearing as an antidote to the potentially catastrophic ecological consequences of the scientific world view.

The shamanic world view seems to have an holistic perspective on the human being, paying equal respect to body, sexuality, emotions, imagination, intellect, and spirit, rather than relying solely on the analytic mind, thus allowing for ambiguity, intuitive insight, direct experience, and empowerment of the individual (Doore, 1988).

Shamans use various tools and strategies for specific purposes. Among the more important ones are power songs, rattles, feathers, and shape shifting. Each shaman will have at least one power song. It is repetitive and relatively monotonous. The song may have the latent function of affecting nervous system activity in a manner analogous to yogic breathing exercises (Harner, 1982).

The oldest musical instrument used for soul retrieval among native people is the rattle, humankind's imitation for rain. It cleanses, purifies, and is used to remedy "soul-loss" (depression or dis-spiritedness). After the shaman cleanses and purifies, he uses the rattle to call back parts of the soul that have been lost in the past, in a particular place, or in a relationship. Higher frequencies to the brain are stimulated by the shaking of the rattle (Arrien, 1993).

Feathers are a direct connection to gods, goddesses, and specific divine forces in some cultures. They are tools for prayer, petitions, and alignment with specific natural forces. They symbolize faith and contemplation (Andrews, 1997).

According to Jamal (1987) the shaman, or shape shifter, is a transformer of things visible and things invisible. In the literal sense, there are shamans who are able to outwardly transform their physical shapes into other forms. Metaphysically, shape shifters can alter their own consciousness and can affect the shape of consciousness of those around them. Thus they are alchemical archetypes.

Shaman means "to heat oneself" and refers to the heat of the Kundalini, which is the inner fire that transforms the ordinary person into the empowered state of the shaman. Kundalini means "coiled up" in Sanskrit, and refers to a potent energy source inherent in all people — a serpent-like energy coiled up at the base of the spine. When this energy is activated, it moves up through the energy centers along the spine and activates healing and psychic powers (Jamal, 1987).

The lost coin may represent the lost part of ourselves, the inferior part that must be recovered if we are to be complete. The coin is to be found in one's own house, that is, within oneself (Sanford, 1987). I place the coin on the altar as an offering of myself.

Summary of Waking Dream 13

Archetype: The Shaman acting on the Physical and Psychological Levels and aligning with:

First Chakra: The shaman helped me to re-connect on a very deep level with the elements of nature. He helped me heal by being in touch with Earth and at the same time, the Spirit. This earth, nature, Spirit, connection has been passed down and is represented by this person who is the priest/healer/prophet/seer/alchemist and keeper of the ancient secrets of transformation.

Fourth Chakra: Emotional Power. Mediating between the body and spirit, the shaman went into my spiritual house and found my lost, very valuable part (coin/power) that had been hidden or lost. This will help me bridge the space between the third and fourth chakras: the point that is sometimes difficult to bridge and one where many people are stuck. This coin (energy) is a part of my soul; that part, when restored to its proper place (an offering on the alter), will be the catalyst for a marriage, a sacred union with myself. The shaman has retrieved a part of my soul and brought it back into the whole. The shaman says that when I express who I am, I am full of power. I possess original medicine unduplicated anywhere. To the shaman, power and medicine have the same meaning. The shaman's way is to gather medicine by reconnecting with oneself on the deepest level.

I believe that this is what happened in this and subsequent images when I was actually the shaman. In all, I experienced about 20 images involving the shaman. This was the first in that series. I included only three in this dissertation.

February 17, 1989

A star blazes across the sky — leaving a long tail that glows brightly. It lights up my spiritual house.

I immediately have a "movie" of all the different kinds of light — out and inner.

"Seek light."

In all religions, light is the major divine symbol (Emmons, 1978).

Sanford (1995) writes that Jung always refers to light as consciousness and when light appears in dreams, it indicates that powerful insights are about to illuminate the consciousness of the dreamer. The psychological sense of the light as a spiritual principle is that it brings consciousness. To belong to the light is to become conscious; to refuse the light is to become unconscious.

As noted in Emmons (1978), several religious writers discuss and describe spiritual light. Jacob Boehme, Christian mystic, talks of light in terms of "an internal light," the "inward center of light" and the "inward light" (p. 100). Underhill describes her inner light as "uncreated light," Divine Light is "Light whose smile kindles the universe" (p. 102). Wescott believes that consciousness itself may be internal "bio-luminescense" or an actual form of light in one's brain (p. 113).

Borg (1995) points out that visions with photism (experiences of light) and auditions (sounds, especially voices) have an especially numinous sacred quality. Villoldo (2000) states that everything living on earth is composed of light. Humans are light bound into living matter. In reality, the body does not produce light, light produces the body. Every living thing is light, bound and packaged in different forms and vibrations. The failure to understand this separates us from the experiences of the Spirit. The body emits energy which is a state of light very close to living matter. It is called bio-plasma, according to contemporary Russian researchers.

Braden (1997) believes that our bodies are encoded through three primary mathematical sequences. They may be considered as literal blueprints of light, bringing to us the code of creation. DNA determines how patterns of light, expressed as matter, surround the body.

Zukav (1989) points out that the frequency of our Light depends on our consciousness. When the level of consciousness is shifted, the frequency of that Light changes. Seeking Light then, is a way of becoming more conscious, with an ability to generate higher frequency Light systems to help heal ourselves, others, our community, and our planet. There is a belief that our species is evolving from one frequency range in the spectrum of nonphysical Light into another, higher frequency range. Thought is energy, also; it is a Light that has been shaped by consciousness. Changing consciousness changes the shape of the Light. This is done with each thought, each emotion, and each intention.

It is interesting that the chakras may be called internal wheels of light. They have a specific frequency and color. On the cosmic level, stars are also another kind of light. They signify the search for Truth. Moving stars indicate the dreamer's search for the Truth amid various spiritual doctrine (Rain, 1990).

Summary of Waking Dream 14

Archetype: Wisdom (Holy Spirit) acting on the Spiritual Level and aligning with:

(I believe the Holy Spirit mediates between my conscious and unconscious mind. Here the Light of the Spirit and the wheels of light align to create new transforming light consciousness.)

All energy centers responded to this message, "Seek light" since they are light themselves. Since this experience occurred in my spiritual house, I am assuming that one specific light to which this message refers is the light of intuition and spirit. Emmons (1978) writes that the inner experience of light has been accorded a high place of importance as religious and spiritual symbolism through the ages. There are approximately 50 direct references to light in the Bible and references to light appear in the sacred texts of every religion.

This image was powerful enough to activate all of the chakras. I believe that one reason for this particular experience was to teach me that everything is connected by light — all kinds — colors, frequencies, uses, on the cellular level and on the cosmic level and that we are responsible for our own light — the Light of Consciousness.

All centers were affected, but the higher chakras, since they are considered spiritual, were those that responded in significant ways:

Fifth Chakra: This center responds to the light of self-control, honesty, spiritualized will and choice and communication of will in a loving way.

Sixth Chakra: These energies open to the light of intellect and reasoning and to spiritually inspired intuition.

Seventh Chakra: These energies open to the light of mysticism and grace, bringing the light of gratitude into every part of life and consciously bringing the light and power of prayers into every moment.

Eighth Chakra: Our energetic connection to The Light draws us like a magnet and makes all other light possible.

May 15, 1989

Note: This was a companion image to 2-2-89 and completed the construction of my spiritual house.

Wise Ones come and say they are ready to help me move into an addition to my spiritual house.

A round room is added to the first floor. The spiral steps leading into the new room are Courage. The room itself is named Consciousness. The walls are Wholeness. The ceiling of glass is Connectedness.

Summary of Waking Dream 15

Archetype: Wise Ones (Holy Spirit) acting on Psychological and Spiritual levels aligning with:

First Chakra: It takes courage to evolve and leave the known for the unknown (new addition). The spiral stairs (courage) is a symbol of growth, especially spiritual growth. The spiraling circle can symbolize the self in the psyche.

Third Chakra: Moving into the new addition (new consciousness), I am invited into more completeness (wholeness, holiness). I understand the sacred truth, All is One, through the connectedness of "my place" with every other person's place. This upper round room may be thought of as a habitable mandala, open and inviting to nature, others, and the Divine.

Sixth Chakra: The balcony represents the gift to see inwardly (insight) and to see outwardly (vision). These realizations carry the sacred truth, Seek Only Truth.

Seventh Chakra: What happened in this experience and is still happening is a complete re-framing or re-structuring or trans-formation of my spirituality. This structure can accommodate the creative movement of the transcendent function that keeps pushing toward individuation and salvation, because the psychological and spiritual journey are the same. In a sense, this dream is a coming home to myself.

Teresa of Avila, 16th century Christian mystic, imagined a castle dwelling to represent the interior spiritual life. She described it this way. "Well, let us imagine that within us is an extremely rich palace, built entirely of gold and precious stones; in sum, built for a Lord such as this .... Imagine, also, that in this palace dwells the mighty King." (Kavanaugh OCD & Rodreguiz OCD, trans. 1979, p. 20)

January 2, 1990

The face of a woman appears. It is an incredible face: strong, leathery but dark, soft skin, lined but with beautiful features, dark bottomless eyes that have seen everything. Ageless, Timeless. It conveys wisdom and compassion. She looks straight at me with a half-smile on her face. She disappears. I am disappointed.

I believe that this image was of the eternal feminine, whatever she is called: mother, goddess, teacher, healer, etc. In particular, this seemed to be the Black Goddess, also called the Black Madonna. Hers is the powerful, earthy aspect of the feminine, a divine force that affects our daily life. This archetype is associated not only with the loving, nurturing side of the feminine, but the other side, the powerful, primal, grounded part. According to Woodman (1996), crusaders brought back Black Madonnas from Africa, and the people revered them, partly because black was associated with wisdom. With the event of the black plague, however, people thought that nature had turned against them, and they suspected that the fault lay with the worship of the Black Madonna (Goddess). Consequently, people projected their shadow onto prominent crones, i.e., Hildegard of Bingen, because someone had to take the blame. Women in general received the demonic projection and thousands of the wisest women were burned as witches. Collectively, women still carry this awful, negative memory energy.

Our understanding of the Goddesses in many forms is much different. There *is* conscious femininity, and it includes the unity and oneness of all of life. Healthy feminism will honor all living things: the power of intuition, the power of prayer, and the power of love. The evolving feminine will strive for flexibility, will care for her body, will care for the environment, and will get out of her head and into love (Woodman, 1996).

As I was forced by illness to slow down, I could welcome the goddess. I could recognize the mystery that my images brought into my life. This archetype with her enigmatic smile and mysterious look was trying to teach me to recognize and celebrate my feminine potential — my creative, intuitive, loving, spiritual femininity that I had all but strangled with my tough rational critic that needed to control, manage, and coerce together with my feeling that I could never be enough or do enough.

Summary of Waking Dream 16

Archetype: Black Goddess acting on the Physical Level and Psychological Level and aligning with:

Second Chakra: Gifts of this chakra honor the feminine creative potential and the ability to work, love, and create with others as partners without the need to control.

Third Chakra: I needed to trust myself and my intuition; to view myself as capable and to celebrate my unique feminine personality (every woman as goddess).

Fourth Chakra: Gifts of this chakra are the ability to give and to receive love and the ability to give and to receive forgiveness. Healthy feminism carries the power of love and the power of prayer.

February 20, 1990

As the Shaman, I am dancing the Shadow Dance. I do all sorts of moves and my shadow sometimes follows, sometimes disappears. At one time, there are two shadows facing each other as though they are starting to box. I am not surprised at anything and dance on.

I receive a verbal message: "It is good to exercise the shadow sometimes."

Sanford (1987) asserts that for all of its darkness, the shadow seems close to God. When we wrestle with our shadows, we wrestle with God. When we dance with our shadows, we dance with God.

The shadow archetype represents that inferior or underdeveloped side of ourselves that has been left behind as we attempt to become as completely rational and moral as possible. It is the uncivilized part of us, the primitive, which is also an essential part. Jung reminds us that this archetype is 90 percent gold when we no longer project it; when we no longer see the shadow in some other person or group who is hated, feared, or glorified. Jung also notes that the shadow can be ten percent evil (Kelsey, 1978). Sanford (1987) points out that the shadow, when given conscious recognition, can add positive value to our personalities: zest for living, earthiness, instinctuality, and humility which we need to become whole.

We are instructed in the Bible to love our enemies: that includes our inner enemy. This means making friends with our inner accuser, and to offer no resistance to that within which we consider evil or inferior or unacceptable to ego standards. This refers to the internal, psychological acceptance of the rejected, negative side of our nature. The inner opponent to our conscious standpoint is to be respected and treated generously. As the shadow is accepted, the wholeness of personality can be approached (Edinger, 1972).

Pascal (1992) notes that sometimes we don't want to make the effort and risk of growth, because confronting the shadow stuff is too hard. Growth must continue, or as Jung suggested, we risk becoming caricatures of ourselves.

The ancients argued that one's shadow was a more or less detachable part of one's soul. The seven souls of the Egyptians included the shadow; and Greeks and Romans said the "shade" was a part of the soul that went to dwell in the underworld after death, deprived of strength, void, and blood. A living person's loss of a shadow, however, was equated with the loss of soul. The Biblical curse, "their shadow has departed from them" (Numbers 14:9, The Open Bible New American Standard) was intended to make enemies into helpless, soulless zombies (Walker, 1988).

I was dancing with my shadow in this experience. Cirlot (1971) points out that dance is the corporeal image of a given process, or of becoming. There is a universal belief that, as an art form, dance is a form of creation which includes a new consciousness.

We are told to seek the gold in the shadow. This must happen as a result of integration, of finding the positive energy behind the negative behavior. What needs to happen is a transformation of old negative habits of mind and the unblocking of negative energy so that positive energy can come in and help the evolutionary process. This archetype helps us to do that (Taylor, 1992).

As I danced with my shadow, I was apparently enjoying the dance and the movement. This is clearly an integration image; the integration of primal, earthy energy into my conscious life. I became aware of the need for more playtime, exercise, more movement of my body, more lighthearted "out of head into body" work. I have always been accused, even as a child, of being much too serious, always careful to do the "proper" thing.

Movement, dancing, and play can be used to open deeper levels of consciousness to the dynamic energies of nature and a realization of greater interconnectedness. I received the message!

Summary of Waking Dream 17

Archetype: The Shadow acting on the Physical Level and aligning with:

First Chakra: I danced a primal dance to help integrate

(exercise) my shadow. This is a healthy way to move in a primal, earthy rhythm feeling the pulse of the earth and nature in the body. It is interesting that I danced as the shaman. This suggests that I needed to be freer in the "exercising" of the first chakra issues. Most women my age do not feel altogether comfortable with their physical, earthy parts because they have been socialized to disregard this "gold," which results in feelings of being victimized or orphaned from their bodies.

All of the chakras' power issues have shadow sides. All stages of consciousness must be aware of shadow elements and be open to how to exercise the shadow side and integrate the gold found there. Therein lies wholeness.

August 19, 1990

I am in a completely white crystal room. Crystals hang from the ceiling and line the walls and floor.

A man with a white beard, white hair, and light robe approaches.

"This is Another Place.

A place of promises kept.

A place of desires realized."

He wears a black, blue, and white crystal necklace which he takes off and places around my neck.

"Wherever you go, the crystals will keep you connected to Another Place. Use its power to help you in your living in your Usual Place."

According to Galde (1988), crystals have long been used for their curative effects when used in preparations of tincture; for their protective characteristics when used as amulets and talismans, and for their ability to enhance the energy fields of the body as they emit uniform vibrations in harmony with the

Mary Jo Davis-Grant

natural vibrations of the human body. Quartz crystals were placed on the native healers' eyes to help him/her become clairvoyant. In certain native tribes, quartz crystals the size of seeds were placed between the bottom two ribs on the left side of the person who was being indoctrinated as a healer. It was removed on the healer's death and placed into a new healer. It was believed that this gave him/her instant all-knowing from his predecessor.

Apache Tear Drop black obsidian crystals are believed to bring good luck, balance emotional states, and protect one from being taken advantage of. They are said to produce clear vision, to increase psychic powers, and to bring to light that which is hidden from the conscious mind. These crystals were thought to create a sometimes radical change in attitude, replacing old negative patterns with new positive ones.

Lapis Lazuli (possibly the blue stones) was thought by some cultures to be a gift from heaven. Ancients believed it to have power of attractions and the ability to garner favor and realize hope. It was also the alchemical symbol of the God within (Galde, 1988).

This image says much and hints much; however, it seems to be clearly saying that there is another realm where wonderful things can happen. Everyone wants desires realized and promises kept. The crystals can help keep the connection to *another place* by enhancing the energy fields of the body as they match the vibrations of the human body. Another connection can be made between them by using the crystals to enhance the intuitive abilities, clear vision, clairvoyance, and in replacing old negative patterns with new positive ones.

Just where *another place* is located is not clear. It could be the collective unconscious which is the storehouse for generations of treasures; it could be an altered state of consciousness

91

where we touch Spirit with all of its gifts. It seems to me that it is a place where, by paying attention to our dreams and symbols, we can stay connected.

Wearing crystals around the neck strengthens all chakras above the waist. Crystals are excellent for increasing visionary powers and increasing faith and spirituality. Again, this image uses a natural, earthy element to help heal and bring the human body, mind, and spirit into harmony and wholeness. I find it particularly interesting that scientists now know that humans carry micro crystals of magnetite in our human brains. They are also in the brains of birds, fish, and honey bees (Shealy, 1999).

Summary of Waking Dream 18

Archetype: Wise One acting on the Spiritual Level and aligning with:

First Chakra: By recognizing and accessing the connection with the natural world (crystals), energy in this center is strengthened.

Fifth Chakra: Boosting higher energies given by the crystals will clarify issues of judgment and knowledge and assist in making wise choices. The Sacred Truth for this center, Surrender Personal Will to Divine Will, is pertinent here.

Sixth Chakra: This center activates the energies of spiritually inspired intuition. An experience like this helps to open one's mind to extravagant possibilities and quiets the demand of rational explanations.

Seventh Chakra: Our connection to the Divine (*another place*) activates the ability to see the larger pattern and the ability to trust life. Faith, inspiration, and humanitarianism are issues here.

Because I believed it would be helpful to ritualize the

image, I learned how to choose my own crystal and attune it to my own spirit.

November 1, 1990

The Great Wise One beckons me off my path. He gives me something liquid out of a hollowed out wooden spoon. He then performs healing by:

placing a rainbow around my head,
capturing and placing sun's rays on my head and stomach.
capturing lightning and placing it in my hands.
placing warm rain on my joints.
moving the earth to adjust my joints.

This treatment feels really good. I feel connected to all of nature, and I am very energized and very alive.

I am reminded that the whole universe can be called on to help us heal. During this particular image I felt so incredibly thankful that I could be experiencing something like this. The Great Wise One was using the gifts (therapy) of the earth and nature to heal, to activate the natural resources in my body. This grounding was solid, natural, earthy. Perhaps the healing was heightened because my feminine biology, psychology, and spirit is responding to the heart, mind, and spirit of Mother Earth. Without this adequate grounding, the hold on the higher energies is tenuous. From a healthy, secure place within, we can connect with feelings, experience body, and truly relate to self and others (Wauters, 1997).

All elements of nature have their source in the spirit world; therefore, they are infused with spirits that can be contacted for any number of purposes, including healing.

Placing a rainbow around my head is a way of aligning and boosting my vibrations with the vibrations of the colors of the chakras. This is color therapy. The rainbow is a symbol of God's protection and covenant.

The sun's rays on head and stomach could be activation of DHEA which is our chemical battery reflecting our life energy reservoir. It is the chemical reflection of Chi. DHEA can be raised within minutes by an accomplished spiritual healer (Shealy, 1999).

Capturing lightning in the hands may be the acceptance and activation of cosmic magnetic energy and the gift of healing (energy work). I started doing energy healing work four years after this image.

The healing benefits of water have been known for centuries. Hot springs and hydrotherapy are well-known and effective treatments. It is interesting that native tribes knew where the natural hot healing springs were, and that area was considered sacred. All friendly and unfriendly tribes gathered here. It was sacred, neutral ground.

The Earth's movement may be nature's chiropractic in action. The magnetic energy present in the earth is probably activated by the earth's movement. This harmonizes and charges the body's energy centers as well as adjusts misalignments.

It is clearly evident that our human physiological, psychological, and spiritual systems are deeply connected and intertwined with the powerfully intense forces of nature and the cosmos. I felt very connected to everything. I realized, again, that All is One.

This feeling of connectedness is another way that the image heals. By entering into the moment and sensing the ecstatic, the truth of being absolutely and totally inseparable from every other aspect of creation is realized. The moment itself is both the definition and the purpose of healing. Sometimes physical problems disappear, and sometimes the patient dies. Either way, with the instant of connection, of unity, healing occurs, according to Achterberg in Doore (1988).

Summary of Waking Dream 19

Archetype: Great Wise One acting on the Physical Level and aligning with:

First Chakra: I felt very safe and secure in the hands of the Great Wise One. I was reminded of the order and structure of nature and how its power is available to us to enjoy and appreciate. I have felt that my biological father's appreciation for nature and his work in conservation were positive tribal attitudes; however, his appreciation for nature often stopped before it included his family. This perception caused me to carry a feeling of insecurity and unworthiness into my adult years.

Using the gifts of earth and nature to activate healing resources in body, mind, and spirit are first chakra gifts. Positive ground building is a necessary base for all energy work. By the date of this waking dream, I had been aware for some time that my first chakra body areas were becoming healthier. I had less pain, more flexibility in my low back, knees and legs and my immune system was stronger. I had few colds, infections and allergies — a great change for me.

November 14, 1990

The Great Wise One is again doing the healing. He moves his hands above my body. A current that feels like electricity moves up and down, following his hands. I tingle and can feel the relaxation and pain relief.

The shaman/healer may use a technique that is something

like a divining rod; with eyes closed, he stretches out his hands back and forth over a patient's head and body, slowly reading the body for sensations of heat, energy, or vibration. By using this technique, the healer gets an indication of where, in what energy center, the energy blockages lie (Harner, 1982).

Some healers call this "finger tip vision." I did not know the concept until 1994 when I started working with a modern shaman, Sam Winters, who uses this technique. During a session with him, I would often feel the energy flowing, see many vivid colors, and have spontaneous images when he worked on my energy centers. Sam's treatments helped keep the fibromyalgia under control. I always felt in a better mood, had less pain and more energy after a treatment, just the way I felt after this image in 1990. I often told him that these tune ups were therapeutic and preventative.

Summary of Waking Dream 20

Archetype: Great Wise One acting on the Physical, Psychological and Spiritual Levels and aligning with all chakras:

The archetype in this waking dream, the Great Wise One, impacted all of the chakras. For optimum chakra functioning, all chakras need boosts of energies. Using the natural magnetism in the hands to maintain the flow of energy is a particularly effective way that one can help assist another to remain well and strong. It is particularly important to keep the first chakra energy flowing. Myss (1995) maintains that all disease starts below the waist in the tribal chakra. A good flow of energy in this chakra will feed the other chakras and provide a necessary grounding for all upper energies.

March 4, 1991

I am walking along in bright sunlight. Suddenly the light changes and the sunlight becomes liquid which spreads like syrup poured out. Then, some of the liquid forms into small drops and enters my body at mid-section. It then spreads to all of my body. I can feel the warmth as the liquid enters my blood stream and is carried to fingertips and tips of toes.

Cirlot (1971) maintains that to ancient alchemists, the sun represented gold. An alchemist concept held that the celestial Sun nourished the inborn fire of man. Jung pointed out that the Sun is, in truth, a symbol of the source of life and ultimate wholeness. Interestingly, the Sun, the nineteenth enigma of the Tarot pack, is related to purification. Its sole purpose is to render the opaque crust of the senses transparent so that they may perceive the higher truths. Apart from providing light and heat, the Sun is the source of supreme riches, symbolized by the *golden drops* which rain down upon the human.

The Sun is considered to be the source of all life: worshiped with sacrifice and elaborate ritual through history by almost every culture in every part of the world. Sun is *the* abiding symbol. In any given period of history and at certain cultural levels, the solar cult is the predominant, if not the only one (Cirlot 1971).

This is another unique healing image involving nature. It reminds me of what I now know about DHEA that I did not know when I experienced this image. DHEA is the chemical battery reflecting one's life energy reservoir, and it is probably the single most important hormone in the human body. DHEA is reduced in every known illness, and it is thought that the decline is related to cumulative stress. Sunlight is critical to the production of DHEA (Shealy, 1999).

Golden drops of liquid sun entered my body at mid-section. Energetically speaking, this is the location of the third chakra, the solar plexus intuition. The source from which our intuition forms its particular data is based on the energy data that is penetrating our own energy system through our solar plexus. This intuition is designed to assist us with survival data. The quality of intuition that operates from this chakra is nature's way of assisting in the process of becoming personally empowered (Shealy and Myss, 1993).

This was a grounding and empowerment image: feeling the body, paying attention, experiencing what is going on in the body, experiencing the connectedness to and nourishment from nature and the elements. I had been in my head so long that I needed to be grounded. I had been sick so long that I needed the filling of the DHEA reservoir to repair and heal my body. The connections between body and spirit are stronger in nature, and I could actually feel the jolt of energy to my midsection and the subtle spreading of warmth throughout my body.

I feel sure that new energy was stored in my mid-section chakra and that the production of my DHEA was stimulated by this image.

Summary of Waking Dream 21

Archetype: The Sun acting on the Physical Level and aligning with:

First Chakra: Issues here are grounding and the connectedness to and appreciation of all of nature.

Third Chakra: One of this chakra's functions is the storage of energy in the solar plexus that feeds all of the chakras.

April 1, 1991

I am being filled.

A kaleidoscope begins with one dot in the center of my body and spreads out until it fills every cell with color, shape, and design.

I am a living mandala.

Pascal (1992) asserts that images of the Self appear spontaneously in dreams and fantasies in the form of symbols of a paradoxical union of opposites. The simplest symbolic form of this squared circle is called a mandala. It is much like a four-spoked wheel. This shape is a symbol of wholeness; it represents an archetypal image of the Self as a reconciliation of all possible opposites. Mandalas come in endless varieties, and their designs are found everywhere, for endless purposes.

"When this Self-symbol emerges in dreams or fantasies, it reflects a transformation of opposites into a higher synthesis, which the uniting mandalic symbol expresses and impacts in a resonating way throughout our whole being" (p. 110). Complicated separate elements of the psyche unite and transcend their differences through the impact of the synthesizing mandala-type symbol. Mandalas are powerful symbols, and their power restores order and harmony, which then permeates all the levels of the psyche. "When these images emerge from the collective unconscious and impact our ego-consciousness, a feeling of deep, profound peace results which is felt as a gift and a grace" (p. 111).

This was the most amazing experience and words fail to describe its perfection and exquisite power. It seemed to me that the mandala was *living me.* An archetypal symbol this strong is a carrier of such meaning and energy that it is capable of re-unifying and renewing our consciousness. Eliade (1991) has made the observation that mandalas can be a technique of mystical physiology. Arrien (1993) calls our body a physiological prism that reflects and absorbs light and can be healed by light and color.

I felt that I was being filled, cell by cell, with glorious color, and I was being turned like a kaleidoscope in the hands of a happy child. As I was being turned, I *felt* colors viscerally. I knew somehow, that I was being fashioned into *just* the right colors, shape, and design: I became this extraordinary living mandala. I felt centered, complete, and unique. I was a one-of-a-kind work of sacred art, created again in a symbolic way that carried such power and promise. I was a prayer. I was holy. I am reminded here of the scripture 1 Corinthian 3:16 (The Open Bible New American Standard), "Do you not know that you are God's temple, and that God's spirit dwells within you? For God's temple is holy and that temple you are."

This wonder happened in an instant, but the shift in perception of what I was and what I had become that was produced is one that changed me forever. Even now, 11 years later, I can relive this rare experience and feel very grateful and still amazed.

Summary of Waking Dream 22

Archetype: Mandala acting on the Spiritual Level aligning and synthesizing with all chakras:

This was a unifying image that produced changes in all of the chakras because each chakra responds to color and movement. The colors with their specific energies flowed into every cell and there were many subtle changes that I will probably never know. This was, I believe, an experience of the "transcendent function" that Jung spoke of and one that can only be lived as a mystery, not understood as an experience.

April 30, 1991

As the Shaman, I deliver a sleeping and dreaming potion to every villager. My village consists of round huts built in a circle around a fire pit. The village sleeps. Before dawn, I awaken each person with a little rattle and they go outside in silence. They draw their dream story in the dirt in front of their huts. Then, they go about getting something to eat and doing their chores — all in silence.

When evening approaches, the whole village gathers around the fire pit and each breaks silence by telling his dream story. I listen carefully and dream elders help me interpret the dreams. This is a very important ceremony or ritual because the welfare of the tribe is foretold by the dreams. This is called the Season of True Dreams.

"Among the Australian aboriginal people, there are big dreams and little dreams. A big dream must not be ignored. It may be big enough to clarify and enlarge your purpose, big enough for you to find the story of your life inside it" (Moss, 1977).

In American Indian cultures, dreams are often part of the religious system. Shamans use their dreams in performing functions such as curing illnesses or divination. Fasting and isolation are two of the various methods for dream incubation, but all of the different rituals lead to the same source of inner wisdom. The dream itself is the most reliable source of guidance in life.

According to Vaughn (1979) the Senoi people of Malaya are noted for the peaceful and co-operative nature of their society. They use dreams on a daily basis for guidance in personal and social affairs. Their children are taught to share their dreams at breakfast, and to control their dreams by lucid dreaming. Dreams are an integral part of daily discussion in the village council, and the tribe's activities are largely determined by their dreams.

Allusions to dreams are abundant in sacred writings of all religions: The Bible has many references to God speaking to man through dreams and visions. The ancient Upanishads refer to dreams as an intermediate state between this world and another, in which death is transcended. In the dream state a person is said to be self-illuminated. The ancient Egyptians believed that divine powers were made known in dreams. The ancient Greeks regarded dreams as instructive and inspirational. A person in search of a healing dream would go to a healing temple, be given a potion by a healer and wait for the god of healing to appear in a dream.

Jung considered dreams to be a bridge between conscious and unconscious processes. "The general function of dreams," writes Jung in Vaughan (1979) "is to try to restore our psychological balance by producing dream material that re-establishes in a subtle way the total psychic equilibrium" (p. 145). Thus, dreams also aid in establishing a balance between rational and intuitive functions.

In my dream, the rattle is used to awaken the tribe. According to Stevens and Stevens (1988) the rattle is an ancient shamanic tool and has been used by shamans on every continent of the world, thus indicating its powerful significance. They are made from dried gourds with beans or pebbles inside, which may have been gathered from some sacred plant or sacred site. Shamans believed that the sound of the rattle aids in opening the doorway to the spirit world. It calls forth the aid of allies and guardians, thus bringing the spirit world and its inhabitants closer to ordinary reality. Rattles were sometimes used as a magicians' wand or directing device as energy is mentally sent through them and out of the sick person's body. It can be used to distribute healing energy within a sick body.

This dream is a teaching parable about shamanic responsibility. Basically, *very basically*, the shaman uses altered states of consciousness to communicate with and influence the forces of nature and the universe for the benefit of the tribe. They explore how to keep things in balance on many levels, and they see disease in terms of disharmony, fear, and soul loss. As Harner points out in Doore (1988), the shaman is a public servant, and in tribal society, her work is for others. She is a kind of spiritual activist by working with powers that connect human beings to the incredible power of the universe.

Other than being a wonderfully refreshing and thought provoking experience, I believe this message was a reinforcement and an affirmation. This dream process was one that I should continue to use for myself and one I should use for the benefit of others. Partly as a result of this dream, I am now intentionally doing dream work with others of my "tribe," my clients, and with groups. I will be teaching a course on dreams next fall or spring at a local college. Something very healthy happens when a group works together in an effort to make concrete through a creative activity something that they were gifted with (the dream). It is one way that dreams can come true. I urge clients and groups to create their dream in some concrete way, i.e., drawing, acting out, writing, or clay.

This dream imagery helps me know just what it costs to be a member of a tribe with all of its responsibilities, rules, and loyalties. To an extent, I felt this with my birth family. A shaman, however, has a specific calling and commitment. It is not an accident of birth. This shift in perspective makes all the difference.

Summary of Waking Dream 23

Archetype: The Shaman acting on the Physical and Psychological Levels and aligning with:

First Chakra: The shaman has responsibility for the physical safety and security for himself and his people. The shaman operates on the assumption that everything is one, her way of stating the sacred truth of this chakra.

Second Chakra: The shaman has control over her tribe, but it is a positive communion *with* them, not over them.

Third Chakra: By giving each person the power to help create tribal well-being, the shaman creates a sense of individuality and self esteem.

Fourth Chakra: The shaman models commitment, caring, and hope as she carefully prepares and administers the dream rituals.

Fifth Chakra: By creating a tribal interconnectedness with the Dream Maker, the shaman surrenders her will to Divine Will for the benefit of the tribe.

May 31, 1991

I fall down in a cave. It is dark but not frightening. I wait and a very small white unicorn comes out of the back of the cave.

"Always consider every possibility. Don't be afraid to consider the unlikely. Everything has meaning."

I fall down into a cave, a place of containment; concealed or enclosed. Because of their darkness, caves are womb symbols. Jung thought caves stood for security and the impregnability of the unconscious. In some myths, caves are the meeting places for archetypes, forebears, or gods and goddesses; they are a place of incubation and introspection. Jung, who studied extensively the relationship between psychology and alchemy, maintained that there are many and various aspects of this fantastic animal, the unicorn. Sometimes the unicorn is transmuted into a dove, sometimes a swordfish or dragon. It is one emblem of the sword or the word of God. Tradition commonly presents it as a white horse with a single horn sprouting from its forehead, but according to esoteric belief, it has a white body, a red head and blue eyes. In China, its skin is five colors: red, yellow, blue, white, and black. Its cry is the sound of bells. In legend it lives a thousand years and is the noblest of animals; however, in antiquity the unicorn appears on occasion with certain evil characteristics. Most cultures do not recognize this negative side of the unicorn and it is sought by many as a symbol of good fortune and good luck (Cirlot, 1971).

Summary of Waking Dream 24

Archetype: The Unicorn acting on the Psychological and Spiritual Levels and aligning with:

This image seems to say: "Be open to knowing what you didn't know you knew. Consider everything on at least three levels."

Fifth Chakra: "Don't be afraid to say what you need to say." By speaking up, making choices and exercising self-control, energy in this center is activated and available for positive action which can serve self and truth.

Sixth Chakra: "Don't be afraid to see what you see." By following hunches and having an open mind to impossible possibilities, energy in this center is reinforced. The spiritual journey is often irrational.

As a woman, I appreciate any activation of these two chakras. Many women doubt their intuition and do not speak up when they need to do so. When this image came to teach me, I was facilitating a group of women survivors of abuse and I had continued my work with a local safehouse. I was needing to speak up, for myself and for those who could not and I needed to follow my intuition. Over the years since 1991, I have been strengthened in these two chakras. Images like this one have helped.

June 7, 1991

I am looking at my pond when I see a snake swimming on the surface. An eagle swoops down, catches the snake in his beak and flies away to his nest. The eagle becomes half snake and they live together for awhile. Then, the eagle becomes himself and flies the snake back, dropping him back into the water. They part as friends.

This was a powerful image involving two very powerful archetypes. Cirlot (1971) gives a long, complete treatment of the snake. Included is Teillard's definition of the snake: "An animal endowed with magnetic force. Because it sheds its skin, it symbolizes resurrection. Because of its sinuous movement, it signifies strength. Because of its viciousness, it represents the evil side of nature" (p. 287).

Philo of Alexandria decided that the snake was the most spiritual of animals. Jung has pointed out that the Gnostics related the snake to the spinal cord and the spinal marrow, an excellent image of the way the unconscious expresses itself suddenly and unexpectedly. In Yoga, the concept of Kundalini, or the snake, is a symbol of inner strength which lies coiled up upon itself in the base of the spinal column. As a result of exercises directed toward spiritualization, the snake uncoils and stretches up through the chakras, corresponding to the various plexuses of the body until it reaches the area of the forehead. At that point, man is said to recover his sense of the eternal (Cirlot 1971).

In Clift and Clift (1992) Jung is quoted as saying, "the idea of transformation and renewal by means of a serpent is a well substantiated archetype" (p. 90). Because of its ability to shed its skin and keep living, the earliest people thought that it lived forever and could heal itself.

Snake dreams often seem to suggest that a person is being presented with a new possibility or that an old attitude or habit or way of life is in the process of transformation. In a dream, the threat of a snake bite may well be indicating a threat of being bitten with a new awareness (Clift and Clift, 1992).

According to Andrews (1997) eagles are symbols of the illumination of spirit, healing, and creation. The eagle brings new vision: This vision may be far reaching to the past, within the present, and to the future. Andrews discusses the attributes, habits, and symbolism of the eagle. Psychologically, eagles are sometimes the symbol of the rediscovery of the inner child who brings a willingness to uncover repressed emotional issues and the courage to explore them. Once they are made aware, childlike purity, creativity, healing, and spirituality can be experienced.

Throughout history, the eagle has been associated with mythology and mysticism in many cultures. There are 59 species of eagles living in almost every country of the world. One of the 59 species is the snake eagle which often has crests of feathers upon its head and whose toes are short and strong to enable them to grasp and hold onto the wiggling snakes. The snake eagle swallows the snake, representing the digesting of higher wisdom, the serpent knowledge.

Native Americans revere eagles: They believe that they are

messengers from heaven and embody the spirit of the sun. To align with eagle medicine is to take on the responsibility and the power of becoming so much more than one appears to be, especially spiritually. Eagle feathers are used in many powerful native healing ceremonies. "White feathers of the bald eagle are especially revered because they are the links to Grandmother medicine, tremendous wisdom, healing, and creation" (Andrews, 1988, p. 138).

A powerful image like this has many possible interpretations on many levels; however, I believe that it is first a powerful integration image: integration on many levels. An archetype of healing, creation, and new higher vision comes from spirit and snatches another archetype out of the primal power center in the unconscious. This archetype symbolizes transformation, transition, wisdom, power, and creativity. Together, they undergo a transmutation and dwell together in harmony for a time of integration and rest. Then, they return back to their own dwelling places, but now they carry great synergistic power which will greatly benefit each.

Summary of Waking Dream 25

Archetypes: The eagle and the snake acting on Physical, Psychological, and Symbolic Levels and aligning with:

Sixth Chakra: This is the location of the "third eye," the spiritual center in which the interaction of mind and psyche can lead to intuitive sight and wisdom. The sacred truth is Seek Only the Truth. Inspiration, creativity and intuitive reasoning are strengths found in this power center.

Seventh Chakra: The gifts of this center are insight into healing, vision, spiritual insight, faith in the Divine presence and the purest form of the transforming energy of grace. The snake creates new life by shedding his skin; we create new life (new consciousness) when we shed old outdated perceptions that no longer serve us. The eagle moves easily between earth and sky. Seventh chakra spiritual power helps move energy all along the chakras, from primal to transformational.

October 21, 1991

I meet three Persons of Light who are colored. One is green, one is red, and one is blue. They represent passionate exhortation, healing, and growth. They approach me singly and hold out boxes of light of each color. As I reach out to take each box, the box and the color disappear into my body. I feel a jolt, then warmth as each becomes a part of me.

Shealy (1999) writes that Valerie Hunt, a UCLA scientist, has spent two decades recording the sounds emitted from the chakras. The music and colors of the spheres may be far more important than one could belief or could dream.

Max Lücher, a German physician, diagnosed personality and mood with color, accomplishing as much as many modern psychometric tests. There is documentation that phototherapy, with various colors, influences beta endorphins, melatonin, serotonin, and protactin. Light affects mood, melatonin, and serotonin. The electroencephalogram follows light frequencies, and trance states are easily accomplished with light (Shealy, 1999).

I didn't realize how amazing this image was until four years later when I learned about the whole energy/color/light concept. One thing about the image stands out. Each of the boxes of color knew exactly where to go in my body. Bruyere (1994) indicates that each specific color vibration must match the particular organ imbalance if it is to be absorbed and utilized by that organ. Whatever color is channeled into the body will be sorted or filtered in an appropriate way by each chakra. Could it be that there was a box that represented each organ, or did the color of the box represent the arbitrary value of each organ and the box of color a "boost," homeopathically for that organ?

Summary of Waking Dream 26

Archetype: People of Light acting on the Physical and Psychological Levels and aligning with:

First Chakra: This image relates to the tribal issues of safety and security for myself, but it also relates to my professional life. I was at this time involved in two projects that involved creating safety and security for others who could not provide for themselves. I trained and supervised volunteers to staff a 24 hour suicide hot-line, and I was on the founding board that created a safehouse for battered women and their minor children.

Fourth Chakra: Creating harmony, being open to new ideas, growth, and healing are the fourth chakra issues. This is the "eye of the needle" where the lower and upper chakras are mediated. All of us need help with this evolutionary process which involves issues of love and forgiveness.

Fifth Chakra: Communication of feelings, creativity, and speaking up for self and others were all issues important in both my inner and outer life. I was actually being called upon for exhortation, healing, and growth for myself and for others as I worked with survivors of abuse and with those in crisis.

January 13, 1992

Along my path, a turtle gives me a ride on its back; then, a raven picks me up and carries me over rough terrain. A snake comes along and shows me a path to take, a badger comes and encourages me to continue, and a bear comes along and takes me to a place of safety so I can rest.

Animals often appear in our dreams where they typically represent our guiding instincts and archetypal patterns. They play a positive role in our psyche and how we relate to them shows how related we are to the Self (Sanford, 1995).

Sams and Carson (1988) have studied the ways of power animals for years. They state that according to the Native Americans, medicine is anything that improves one's connection to the Great Mystery and to all of life. This includes healing of body, mind, and spirit. This medicine is also anything which brings personal power, strength, and understanding. Native American medicine is an all encompassing way of life for it involves walking on the Earth Mother in perfect harmony.

Animals exhibit habitual patterns that will relay specific messages of healing to anyone aware enough to observe their lessons on how to live. "The priceless gifts of true medicine are free, and each animal in creation has lessons to impart; all of those lessons are powers that can be called upon" (Sams and Carson, 1988, p. 13). Animals can speak in a special way, the way of power. Certain animals may carry special medicine, power medicine. This special power comes from the idea of unity and of each being having within itself a part of all other beings. It is the law of oneness.

From this holistic perspective, this image takes on special meaning. Again, from Sams and Carson (1988) comes an understanding of specific power animals:

Turtle is personification of the goddesses of energy and the creative force within. Turtle is the symbol of primal matter and is a fine teacher of the art of grounding. "Turtle is the oldest symbol for planet Earth" (Sams and Carson, 1988, p. 77).

"Throughout time the *raven* has carried the medicine of magic" (Sams and Carson, 1988, p. 101). Raven is the guardian of ceremonial magic and in any healing circle, he is present. Raven guides the magic of healing and change in consciousness that will bring about new reality and will dispel disease and illness and bring in a new state of wellness (consciousness).

The power of *snake* is the power of transmutation symbolized by its life-death-rebirth cycle. When snake energy of wholeness reaches spirit level, it becomes wisdom, understanding, wholeness, and connection with Great Spirit. "The power of snake medicine is the power of creation, for it embodies sexuality, psychic energy, alchemy, reproduction and ascension (or immortality)" (Sams and Carson, 1988, p. 61).

The power of the *badger's* medicine is aggressiveness and willingness to fight for what it wants. Keepers of the medicine roots, badger people, are the finest healers and will use unconventional ways to find a cure. Badger medicine may be saying that one is too meek.

The *bear* symbolizes the power or medicine of introspection. To become like the bear and enter the safety of the womb-cave, one must attune the self to the earth energies, receive nourishment, quiet the mind, and find answers while dreaming. Female receptive energy that allows visionaries and mystics and shamans to prophesy is contained in bear energy. From the cave of the bear, the pathway to the other levels of imagination or consciousness may be found. "To accomplish the goals and dreams that we carry, the art of introspection is necessary" (Sams and Carson, 1988, p. 57).

This image really made me think in a new way and be open to new possibilities. I knew nothing of power animals, but as I studied the concept, I was amazed to find that it carried meaning for me, and that it was quite appealing. There is validity to this belief that all of nature can teach.

Summary of Waking Dream 27

Archetypes: Power Animals acting on Physical, Psychological, and Spiritual Levels and aligning with all chakra transitions:

All Chakras: The alchemist raven picks me up and "carries" me into another consciousness. The raven energy carries one from one consciousness to another, in effect, assisting in the transitions from one energy center to another, and helping to overcome difficulties that all kinds of transformation incurs. His energy thus carries magic and mystery because this evolutionary process *is* one of spiritual mystery. The caution is to use this strong energy in a positive way.

First Chakra: Issues addressed are those of attunement with feminine earth energies within the place of safety. The bear took me to a place of introspection, safety, and security so that I could rest and re-charge. Providing a place of safety and rest for survivors is part of my work.

The turtle with its primal, grounding energies carried me and provided me with the way to move ahead, centered and strong. Turtles also carry the ancestor tablets of wisdom. Issues of grounding and primal power and honoring the creative force within are in this chakra. I recognized that I need to keep grounded and am making an effort to spend time in the natural world. I remind myself often that the Sacred Truth of this chakra is All Is One.

Fifth Chakra: The badger brought me the energy of persistence and the ability to stand up for myself. Issues here are lovingly communicating one's will and refusing to be a victim. I do not consider that I speak woundology but I do, on occasion, let others take advantage of me (Myss, 1996). I need to be ever aware of that tendency and "unplug" from that. I need to be able to speak up for others who are victims.

Sixth Chakra: When the springtime comes (rejuvenation and rebirth), bear energies help to give visionaries and mystics the female receptive energies that they need to produce new life and new consciousness. The snake gives wisdom to select the right path. Creativity and evaluation of conscious and unconscious insight, creation spirituality and the loving uses of intuition and wisdom are issues here. Snake energy is also healing energy.

April 8, 1992

In prayer: "A mother's love is a bridge of light over the abyss."

July 13, 1992

Verbal message:
    Truth is
    Love does
    Speak *the truth*
    Do *the love*

Amerson (1999) in a sermon found on the Internet quotes Teilhaard de Chardin:

Love is the only force that can make things one without destroying them .... Someday after mastering the winds, the waves, the tides and gravity, we shall harness for God the energies of love, and then, for the second time in the history of the world, man will have discovered fire.

Shealy (1999) writes:

Since the discovery of electricity, electromagnetism has been seen to be the foundation for life energy itself. Although metaphysical oriented individuals describe a fourth dimensional energetic system, currently there is no measurable fourth dimensional energy system. Someday this fourth dimensional energy, often referred to as love, will be harnessed, but at least at present, spirit and divine love cannot be measured .... Ultimately, love is the greatest spiritual attitude. Love means not necessarily liking to nurture or help others without conditions or reward, but desiring to do so nevertheless. Unconditional love without judgment, with no need to know why, is often said to be the essence of Christian faith or of God. (p. 83)

Prayer is like a magnet; it draws divine energy and focuses it. Unconditional love is also a magnet; it draws divine energy and focuses it. Together prayer and love are very powerful energies because the power of God, the light of God, creates a bridge between the prayer, the love, God, and the person who is prayed for. This is the kind of power that can bridge the abysses of life.

These were two of several of my "auditions" or "locutions" or image-less messages. Auditory imagery involves music or words, but can also include stronger forms, i.e., roaring, crying, buzzing, etc. It can sometimes be more powerful than visual imagery (Vaughan, 1979).

Teresa of Avila (Kavanaugh OCD & Rodreguiz OCD trans. 1979) speaks of intellectual visions, locutions, or auditions and notes their characteristics:

- They are very clear and very compelling.
- They come even when one is thinking about something else.
- Their words are different; one could not compose them so quickly.
- Often, there is much more to understand than is ever dreamed of without words.
- They come with unmistakable power and authority.
- They leave the soul quiet.
- They remain in memory a long time.
- They come with assurances of fulfillment.

Borg (1998) notes that in non-ordinary states of consciousness that mark these experiences of audition and sounds, especially voices, reality is experienced as more than the visible world of our ordinary consciousness. These experiences have a poetic quality to them; they involve a knowing, not simply a feeling. They are said to be numinous, sacred, from the world of spirit.

Summary of Waking Dream 28

Archetype: Wisdom (Holy Spirit) acting on the Spiritual Level and aligning with:

Fourth Chakra: Zukav (1989) writes that an authentically empowered person lives in love, that love is the energy of the soul and that love is what heals the personality. There is nothing that cannot be healed by love. There is nothing but love; it is the richness and fullness of your soul flowing through you. He states: "Humbleness, forgiveness, clarity and love are the dynamics of freedom. They are the foundations of authentic power" (p. 233).

All issues concerning love, including creating from the heart are centered here in the transfer point between the lower body frequencies and the higher chakra frequencies. The Sacred Truth of this center is Love is Divine Power.

Fifth Chakra: Speaking truth, being honest in thought, deed, and relationship, involve going beyond the love feeling and making the conscious choice to *do* love unconditionally. Here is the call to surrender personal will to divine will and realize that true authority comes with aligning personal will with God's will. This is where one makes the choice of faith over fear and enhances the upper chakra energies.

Seventh Chakra: Mysteries, grace and one's connection with the Divine are energies in this chakra. Prayers for self and others are stored here; they become bridges of light for those for whom we pray. These energies become stronger as connections to God's Divine Energy become stronger and miracles happen — miracles like answered prayers.

The several locutions that I have experienced have made tremendous impact. They are indelible; I will remember them always. They are recorded in my mind and on my heart and shift my perception in an instant and raise my consciousness in a heartbeat. They come as a grace and I often feel moved to tears by their message.

April 14, 1992

Many angels are around me weaving many different colors. They seem to be the color they wear. They even carry that particular color. They treat my body with different colors in different places. Then, they stand me before a panel of colors. It is very high and very wide. I see nothing but the wall of color (in strips). Angels ask me to choose colors. I take certain long strips of color from the wall and place them on my body. After I have several, angels touch me and the colors and the angels spin together in a vortex and enter my body.

I am to live the colors; *as I do, I am healed.*

"Phototherapy with various colors influences beta endorphins, melatonin, serotonin, and age of sexual development" (Shealy, 1999, p. xvi).

Bruyere (1994) has studied extensively chakras, color, sound and vibration. Her findings indicate that each chakra has a specific color and a specific sound. Chakra harmonics are varying frequency bands of the same color or wave form. Thus, the auric field actually exists in different layers of color. For people who can see the aura, it appears as a pattern of colors near the body and then another pattern of colors farther away from the body, and so on.

"Vibration, color, and sound are all interrelated and all three represent a means of determining or monitoring the frequency of energy in the auric field" (Bruyere, 1994, p. 63). When a healer is channeling energy into a person, the healer will often feel a vibration within his muscles. This vibration is directly related to the color being channeled. Thus, the healer can sense the color of energy being channeled into the body.

Research conducted by Dr. Valerie Hunt at UCLA did scientifically match color to sound; vibration and color correlated directly. Furthermore, their research equipment was able to measure seven (and there may be more) harmonics or varying frequency bands of sound, vibration, and color of each chakra. When treating an illness by healing with energies, an imbalance of any color can be treated, corrected, and enhanced with its opposite or complimentary color.

Certain body organs respond to specific colors. Each chakra, in fact, contains both its primary color and its color opposite. Whatever color is channeled into the body will be sorted or filtered in an appropriate manner by the chakra. As the energy moves up the system, each chakra takes the energy being received and sorts out the particular color (frequency) needed in that area.

Bruyere (1994) continues: Since ancient literature refers specifically to the chakras as projections of energy (manifested as different colors) healers have agreed that an understanding of the endocrine system will lead us to an understanding of the proper relationship of color and light to the chakras and thus to the endocrine secretions and the production of hormones. Energy healing is interrelated to and cooperative with these biochemical messengers because of the chakra-endocrine connection.

Shealy (1995) stated in a lecture that on the cosmic level, the chakra frequencies respond to solar frequencies specifically. Thus, our bodies need to receive regular sunlight and natural light so that the chakras can be activated and can function efficiently.

Angels are referred to 300 times in the Bible, and we are told that God has countless angels at His command. Graham (1975) states that he "is convinced that these heavenly beings exist and that they provide seen and unseen aid on our behalf" (p. 23).

Missions of and appearances of angels are referred to 74 times in the Gospels and Acts. The word angel is derived from the Greek word for messenger. It means, in both the New and Old Testaments, one of the host of spirits that wait upon some spiritual ruler, some divine monarch. They can be and are messengers or instruments and vessels of higher spiritual reality (Kelsey, 1978). Psychologically speaking, whenever we consciously encounter a divine agency which assists, commands or directs us, we can understand it as an encounter of the ego with the self (Edinger, 1972).

This image was enchanting. I loved the idea of colored angels carrying specific colors to me and becoming healers by swirling into my body, bringing the specific colors needed by each energy center. I was to heal by the colors becoming a part of me, a vital internal rainbow of color designed to energize me. As I lived the colors, I healed. Later when I learned about chakras, I was *truly* amazed by this image!

Summary of Waking Dream 29

Archetype: Angels as Healers acting on the Spiritual Level and aligning with:

(I am interested that the angels asked me to choose colors. I believe that they were strengthening and honoring my intuition. I remember choosing intuitively yellow and blue, colors related to chakras three and five.)

Third Chakra: Control over self and others, self-criticism and perfectionism are issues in this personal power chakra.

Fifth Chakra: Communication of feelings, creativity and releasing personal will to Divine will are issues in this chakra.

These have been and continue to be issues that I must continually evaluate. I still bear symptoms that relate to those two energy centers, but I am much, much better. When I went to the pain clinic, much of my pain was in my lower and middle back and in the neck and shoulders. I felt as if I were personally carrying the weight of the world on my shoulders and I could not seem to communicate my concerns or my will. Having been gifted by images such as this one helped me trust my personal will to the Divine Will and to remain open to all possibilities, as extravagant or irrational as they may seem. As I learn, I heal from the inside out.

March 3, 1993

I am in a church sanctuary. I'm conscious of angels milling around. They seem to be making sweeping motions with their arms (wings). They tell me that they are sweeping out "all that is unholy."

"He will give his angels charge of you, to guard you in all your ways" (Psalm 91:11 The Open Bible, New American Standard).

This image makes me chuckle now as it did when I first saw it. The idea of angels busily sweeping out all that is unholy from a church seems humorous to me. They were, however, quite serious about this work. For about one year, I experienced many kinds, sizes, and purposes of spiritual beings. I have included only a few in this writing. While humorous, this image has impact psychologically and spiritually.

Graham (1975) believes angels are watching; they mark our path. They overlook the events of our lives and protect the interest of the Lord God, always working to promote His plans and bring about His highest will for us.

Howard (1992) asserts that angels are creations of light; when seen in visions or meditations, they usually appear in bright, radiant, stirring, ethereal form. They appear as glowing beings of light with radiating auras that possess such a dynamic energy that they can actually merge with our own energy. They have force centers and lines of energy within their bodies of light.

Howard (1992) also states that angels are actually "living prayers" and prayer is an activity of creation. Zukav (1989) believes that through their service to humanity, angels become the energy of prayer in action and expression. Angels amplify, magnetize, and multiply prayer requests to God. Angels are nonphysical teachers. This is not their home, but they teach here. The angelic kingdom is their home and the numerous beings who live there are of numerous frequencies and qualities of consciousness; many guide and interact with us on Earth. Evolution continues in their realm. "An angel may be thought of as a force of consciousness that has evolved with an appropriate teaching modality for village Earth but may also have been a part of evolution of other galaxies and life forms there" (p. 4).

"Call angelology 'theology-fiction' or 'philosophy-fiction' or regard it as a legitimate part of theology as queen of the sciences, with philosophy as her handmaiden." (Adler, p. 4, 1982)

Summary of Waking Dream 30

Archetype: Angels as Protectors acting on Spiritual Level and aligning with:

Seventh Chakra: Faith, courage, inspiration and spirituality are seventh chakra energies. The Sacrament here is Extreme Unction which reminds that any unfinished business or unresolved issues need to be resolved so that the present time is filled only with love. Perhaps the angels are helping to sweep out all that is unholy in my living temple, removing all that is unholy from my body, mind, and spirit. Adler (1982) asserts that the Powers, a certain order of angels, are those that protect us from all evil influences.

June 26, 1993

Three People of Light come to me on slanted beams of amazing light. I cannot understand what they are about for a time. They explain that they are spiritual ones who "arrange" the answers to prayers. They arrange coincidences, synchronic-

ities, and amazing graces. Sometimes, they can arrange things quickly; sometimes it takes longer; sometimes they cannot at all. There are many considerations when/as/if/before/after they do the answering.

They take my requests and the image fades, but it is one that stays there on my visual screen for a long time.

I had long pondered how prayers are answered. I know that they are, and we are invited to pray without ceasing. A prayer should be prayed with faith and joyous expectation, and then we need to let go of the results.

This image was helpful in giving me a context into which I could let go. This kind of prayer central or God-space interface was a wonderful, whimsical way to gain some detachment and let God be God, angels be angels. I could pray and then be on about my work. In a manner of speaking, we can say that all time and all space are accessible to us in prayer; and in another way, we can say that there is neither time nor space in prayer (Ulanov and Ulanov, 1982).

Zukav (1989) maintains that intercessory prayer pulls us into the tow of God's connectedness to everything. We are pulled into a current that shows us nothing is separated from anything else, no one from everyone else. Prayer is moving into personal relationship with Divine Intelligence. It is impossible to have a prayer without power. "When you pray, you draw to you and invoke grace which is uncontaminated conscious light. It is Divinity. Prayer brings grace, and grace calms. It calms with a sense of knowing" (Zukav, 1989, p. 241).

Summary of Waking Dream 31

Archetype: Spiritual Beings acting on the Spiritual Level and aligning with:

First Chakra: I continued to reframe my early religious

teachings about the approachability, function, and appearance of angels. On another level, this image underscored the sacred truth "All is One" beautifully. This is also where I can do something positive to impact my family, for I can pray always when I can do little else for my grown children and their families. For me, prayer is a tribal imperative.

Fourth Chakra: The heart chakra is concerned with issues of love, compassion, and the recognition that the most powerful energy we know is love. More than any other, this is the "let go and let God" center where all intercessors are challenged. The sacred truth, so applicable here, is Love is Divine Power. Zukav (1989) writes that the loving personality seeks not to control, not to dominate, but to empower. Love is the richness and fullness of one soul flowing to others.

Seventh Chakra: The Divine connection contains the energy that generates devotion, inspiration, prophetic thoughts, and transcendent ideas. This is the entry point for the human life force which pours into the human life form from God. Prayers are warehoused here, and this is where we allow our spirituality to become an integral part of our physical lives, where we allow it to guide us, and where we ask the angels to guard us in all our ways.

August 23, 1994

I am aware of a deep, deep relaxation and altered state. Then, I see a Cloud of Witnesses all around me. I am completely surrounded — most are females.

"We are here to help you to understand the cause of much grief and pain. It is time to forgive. Can you forgive? Even your family?

I decided that I really wanted to forgive but did not know if

*I could. An angel came close and gave me the energy I needed
to really forgive, and I answered, "Yes."*

*"You understand that you are not just forgiving for yourself
but for all the other similar kinds of dis-eases caused and felt
through the generations. That way, generations can be healed
and genetic ribbon lines cleansed.*

*"The secret of long life and health is not only a healthy
lifestyle but also cleansing of this genetic ribbon. This ribbon or
tape or strand gets kinks in it where there is a genetic injury,
i.e., abortion, miscarriages, depression, suicides. It is a spiritual
exercise. True healing cannot happen any other way."*

*I was shown from above a long female genetic line or rib-
bon with various knots, twists, kinks in it. Then, I watched as
my forgiveness was applied to them and the kinks were
released. I was aware that there were releases in my body at
the same time.*

*When it was time for the healing for the male line, I
paused. An Angel of Acceptance came, helped me to use her
energy, and the process was repeated.*

Often, dreams reveal not only forgotten parts of ourselves,
but also inherited and undiscovered parts within the psyche
(Kelsey, 1978).

Philosopher Miguel de Unamuno reminds us of the
importance of ancestral connections and the help that is
deeply rooted within us. "All my ancestors live undiminished
in me and will continue to live, united in me, in my descen-
dants" (Arrien, 1993, p. 114).

In *Water and the Spirit*, Somé (1994), who is from West
Africa, states that he believes the restlessness that traps the
modern individual has its roots in the dysfunctional relationship with the ancestors. Ancestors have an intimate and
absolutely vital connection with the world of the living in

many non-western cultures. They are always available to teach, guide, and to nurture. Representing one of the pathways between the knowledge of this world and the next, relationships between the two must be kept in balance or chaos results. If an imbalance exists, the Dagara believe it is the duty of the living to heal their ancestors; and in the healing, they heal themselves.

In the image, I wanted to forgive, but I did not know if I could. An angel came close and gave me the energy I needed to know that I could. Through this imaging process, I have been taught that some angels *are* the quality they carry. They come into our space and give *us* their energy, enabling us to do what we need to do. They actually change the energy field.

MacNutt (2000), a former Catholic priest who has long been a leader in Christian healing writes:

> One area of prayer for healing that is particularly appropriate to consider during this period in history is generational healing. When I first heard about healing in the 60's, I didn't hear anything about generational healing, but in recent years more and more leaders in the healing ministry have discovered how important it is for most peoples lives, including their own. As we look to the future, it is important for us to consider our past. (p. 1)

He continues by pointing out that we know that physical traits and illnesses can certainly be passed down from generation to generation. We also know that spiritual generational influences can affect us, for both good and evil. Patterns of "dis-ease" as well as pattern of "ease" can run through families for we are the recipients of both positive and negative generational attributes and influences. MacNutt believes that the first step in the healing process is to recognize how our family history affects us. Then, we can bring the bondages to prayer, praying for forgiveness and for release of their effects on us and generations to come. At the same time, we bring the positive gifts for celebration (MacNutt 2000).

This image confirmed a new possibility for ministry for me. Since I work with women who have been abused, I often encounter patterns of generational abuse. After researching this subject of generational healing, I have used this very powerful spiritual process as an integral part of my own healing work and in my private and group work. The results have been astounding.

Summary of Waking Dream 32

Archetype: Spiritual Beings acting on the Spiritual Level and aligning with:

First Chakra: Developing and maintaining a healthy pride in one's ancestry and in family loyalty and love create positive energy. As one takes responsibility to be a healer, healing happens for that one, too. Intercession is needed for all our family, living or not.

Fourth Chakra: The heart is the "eye of the needle" between the lower and upper chakras. One must move through the heart and deal with issues of unconditional love and forgiveness. No further progress on the spiritual journey can be achieved until these issues are resolved, including personal *and* ancestral love and forgiveness issues that may require that we extend ourselves for the good of all, including future and past generations.

Sixth Chakra: By having an open mind to irrational possibilities, power is activated in this chakra. Certainly, some might call generational healing irrational; nevertheless, I have witnessed the effectiveness of this form of intercessory prayer.

Seventh Chakra: This chakra is the connection with mysticism and the Divine. Prayers for self and others are stored here. As one comes to regard life as a vehicle for spiritual development, energy in this chakra is reinforced. Fox (1988) maintains mysticism brings harmony and balance to our bodies, brain and psyche. Perhaps he was referring to the energies of this chakra.

Meinrad Craighead in Bancroft (1989) has made a particularly pertinent observation in regard to the connections between generations. "We are born connected. What layers of your mother's did you imbibe in the womb, and what memories of hers entered you before you were born" (p. 23). Craighead also states:

> I am born remembering rivers flowing from my mother's body into my body. I pray at the fountain of life, saturated in her milk and blood, water and honey. She passes on to me the meaning of religion because she links me to our origin in God the Mother. (p. 14)

December 12, 1994

I am connected to something that looks like an umbilical cord. I look like a semi-solid cloud or spirit floating in a vast light space. I float there until I begin to be "regressed" — something like a VCR re-winding. I see my family, places and people in my history and think that I am going to have a birthing experience. I see my parents as they must have looked when I was born. I did not stop there. I went much further back until I realized that I was being born — spiritually. This is my spiritual conception. The umbilical cord attaches me to God and I am still attached to God and I will always be attached to God. "That's the way it is."

I receive spiritual nourishment, spiritual life through the cord and I am dependent on this connection for my "be-ing." I am constantly re-created and it will always be so. I can never be un-created spiritually.

Breathe on me breath of God

Fill me with life anew

That I may love what thou dost love

And do what thou wouldst do.

(Breath On Me Breath of God, The United Methodist Hymnal, 1989)

The Hebrew word for Spirit is Ruach which means both wind and breath. Both are suggestive, both are invisible but manifestly real. The wind blows, it is all around us. Breath is like wind inside the body. Symbolically, God as Spirit is both wind and breath. Our breath is God breathing us, and God is as near as every breath. Speaking of God the Spirit as both wind and breath evokes both transcendence and nearness (Borg, 1998).

In Indian speculation, the air has woven the Universe by linking together this world and the other world and all beings, as it were, by a thread just as the breath (prana) has woven human life (Eliade, 1991).

Wolf (1996) writes that the Qabalists, Jewish mystics, recognize that there are three symbols that were considered primary to existence and the nature of human consciousness. These symbols are called the "mother-letters." They are aleph, mem, and sheen.

According to this ancient wisdom, the Spirit or God or Aleph, first breathed a cloud into the universe. This cloud resisted anything else that God or Aleph might produce. This resistance allowed whatever else God was to breathe and reflect back. As this reflection took place, consciousness was born in the universe.

Biblical scholar Carlo Suares explains that the universe is Spirit projecting itself, tending to become aware of itself, by emanating a cloud of consciousness on which it can self-reflect. Gradually, energies appear, one coming from the source of consciousness and the other from the cloud as a reflection; thus, allowing itself to be realized. Qabalists understood sheen as the breath of God or as Spirit itself (Wolf, 1996).

In one culture, a cord is seen as a connector between heaven and earth (Kelsey, 1991). The umbilical cord reaching to heaven is an explicit image of the ego, self axis (Edinger, 1992).

January 2, 1995

I am connected to God by the spiritual umbilical cord. I can never be un-created and separated from God. I can, however, improve or neglect how well the nourishment and creativity can flow through the cord. My job is to breathe in deeply, visualizing as I breathe in, how God's strength, wisdom, love, guidance, healing — the total spiritual life force — enters my body, mind, and spirit. As I exhale, I send this life and wholeness to every cell in my body. In this way, every cell is fed and re-created every time, every breath. God expects me to be a co-creator with her of my own wholeness.

Braden (1997) points out that non-destruction of consciousness is the law of creation; you cannot separate or un-create that which is eternal. It is this indestructibility of the eternal soul that provides the momentum to continue the life experience. One is aware on a deep level of the eternal nature of consciousness; it is encoded within the patterns of light memory that reside within each cell of the human body. Eternal life is based within eternal truth; an absolute within each cell of the code of creation. This force within is eternal and cannot be destroyed. Life is the expression of that force.

Foster (1992) speaks of the breath prayer in which we are asking God to show us His will, His way, His truth for our present need. The breath prayer is discovered more than created. It is short, simple, and can be spoken in one breath. The familiar Jesus Prayer is one example of breath prayer. Wolf (1996) believes that one can think of prayer as reaching out to the future. Soul-talk responds when prayer is reversed so that time reversed messages and prayers coincide.

Unceasing prayer becomes prayer with every breath, affecting the past, present, and future. This is the spirit in which this image and this message came to me. As I breathe in, God's strength, wisdom, love, guidance, healing, the total spiritual life force enters my body, mind, and spirit. As I exhale, I visualize sending God's wholeness to every cell in my body. I am re-created with my every breath. God and I are in sacred relationship; we are co-creators of my wholeness.

I have always believed that we are created spiritually before we are created biologically; even so, this image was mind boggling to me. As I considered it over the next months and years, I could only marvel at its power that is hard to convey in words. Now, six years later, the power is still there, and I see that umbilical cord with my spiritual eyes, and I am grateful beyond words for the image and its message. It has strengthened both my spiritual perception and my spiritual understanding. Both are necessary for learning symbolic sight.

Summary Waking Dream 33 (two preceding)

Archetype: The Umbilical Cord acting on the Spiritual Level and aligning with:

Sixth Chakra: Gifts of intellect and reasoning are found here. When I was being regressed, I had to still my fear and work on detachment. It seems to me that this image caused a synergy between mind, spirit, and psyche that led to spiritual intuitive sight. I could then receive the wisdom of the message and this Binah energy of Divine understanding then could create physical results. I feel that an experience of this nature cannot be expressed through a system of written or spoken language and so must come as an image. A Zen koen says it best, "If you can say what it is, that's not it" (Myss, 1996, p. 252).

Seventh Chakra: This center of mysticism and grace is our spiritual connection and our capacity to allow spirituality to guide us. It is also the prayer center and my breath brings the Spirit life force into my human energy system through the umbilical cord. This "breath of God" pours into the physical body and the lower chakras, connecting the entire body to this spiritual energy center. In this way, my spirit remembers always that I am forever with the Spirit. This chakra energy seeks and maintains a connection to the Divine in everything I do, in every breath I take. This is my understanding of how I can become a true co-creator with God.

This kind of connection with God has very little to do with organized religion: It is an *individual* experience and responsibility in pursuit of an intimate relationship with the Divine. For me, this experience continued the re-structuring and transformation of my spirituality. Where my spiritual house experience was on one structural level, this one is on an entirely different, more intimate relational inner level.

March 3, 1995

This image begins a series of seven images about My Bridge.

I am standing on the bank of a beautiful river. Angels in all colors are behind me. They say that I need to move from this side "Known" to the other side of the river "Unknown." I am at a loss to know how I can get across this wide river and begin to plan how I might possibly accomplish this when I notice that the angels are beginning to build a bridge. They say that there is no permanent bridge because each person who crosses has a unique bridge to cross — one made especially for her. They work quickly and I am astonished at the beauty, the grace, and the strength of the bridge. I begin to cross and the bridge becomes even longer, higher, and more beautiful as I proceed.

Arrien (1993) writes that in shamanic societies, symbols are bridges between visible and invisible reality and are the psychological mechanisms for transforming energy. Shamanic traditions believe that our own symbolic structures contain divine revelations. Journeys are seen as teaching tools that provide healing, teaching, and visions and it is important to trust the psyche's wisdom and simply observe what is revealed during the journey, not to direct or control the process.

Summary of Waking Dream 34

Archetypes: Angels and My Bridge acting on the Physical and Spiritual levels and aligning with:

(This waking dream is the first of a seven dream series that indicated the completion of a cycle and a major transition into another cycle.)

First Chakra: The angels (divine guidance) invited me to evolve (become more conscious) by moving from the security and safety of the known to the riskiness and vulnerability of the unknown. I stood undecided because I did not possess the physical power (energy) to cross the river (challenge) without external help (dependence on group or tribe). I did, however, begin to consider how I might accomplish this (am open to possibilities). This dream did not come to tell me what I already knew or ask me to do what I already could do. In the challenge was the gift.

Seventh Chakra: Angels told me that each person's bridge (vehicle for evolution of consciousness) is unique and that each must be fashioned according to the purpose for which the person was created (according to one's sacred contract).

I stepped out in faith into the mystery of the unknown. I paused to appreciate the creative strength and the grace that supported me (connection to my divine creator), and I gave thanks for my sacred journey.

May 1, 1995

I am on My Bridge — angels before me and behind me. We meet a spiritual being (Jesus?). He says that he will "keep" all of my concerns (people, things, and situations) for me. I am to go ahead along my bridge.

Two angels (really powerful) one feminine, one masculine, are to be my special guides for this portion of my journey. I look back and see all I'm concerned with in a circle of light.

I step ahead. I find that I have to go up two or three steps that are in my way. I see that we are very high above streams, hills, and wilderness below. Above is a wonderful light, coming down over us.

Sanford (1995) believes that "the whole process of the examination of one's life and the analysis of one's dreams, which psychological analysis employs to assist in the process of individuation, is an exercise in living in and by the Light" (p. 101). The Light comes from a deeper reality than the ego; it is that which enlightens and greatly expands consciousness. To belong to the Light is to become conscious. "Becoming conscious, living in the Light, is hard work" (p. 105).

Summary of Waking Dream 35

Archetypes: Spiritual Beings, My Bridge acting on Physical and Spiritual levels and aligning with:

First Chakra: It was difficult to "unplug" from the safety and security of tribal paths and step up into the mystery of a new path.

Fourth Chakra: Although I was on my way, I was still concerned about the external, people, things, and situations (loyalties, control by and of others). A spiritual being took these concerns and placed them in the Light. I gave up control because I love my family and friends enough to let them experience their world in their own way. I gave up my control and moved beyond their control.

My guides represented the opposites in my psyche. They were to accomplish some integration, perhaps a marriage of soul and self.

May 10, 1995

Angels ahead on My Bridge invite me forward. "It is even better the further you go. Come on."

In the view of the Bible, angels, visions, and dreams are all part of the same reality. Scholastic theologian Thomas Aquinas had an interest in the reality of angels. He described an angel as "a thought that thinks itself" (Clift and Clift, 1992, p. 65).

Braden (1979) writes that one person who allows for a new possibility becomes a living bridge, both a pioneer and a midwife, for every person who will have the courage to choose the same new path. Each time the individual makes the same choice, that choice becomes easier, then easier for the next and easier for the next.

Summary of Waking Dream 36

Archetypes: Angels, My Bridge acting on the Spiritual level and aligning with:

Fifth Chakra: This chakra carries gifts of choice, consequences and the knowledge that honesty of thoughts and beliefs carry energy. I chose to continue my spiritual journey, accepting Divine guidance.

Sixth Chakra: I have now made my choice and I have attached my will to that of the divine guides. They seemed to be coaches, urging me on and helping me to open my mind to new possibilities. I was rather amused by the angels' excitement over showing me the new possibilities.

May 20, 1995

On my bridge, we come to a golden-looking person who is seated at a small table or desk. I ask, "Am I going to have to pay a toll to go on over my bridge?"

The person hands me a coin (I think) and says, "You will need this further on. It is the coin of the realm."

Summary of Waking Dream 37

Archetypes: Spiritual Being, My Bridge acting on the Spiritual level and aligning with:

Third Chakra: I found that I had the personal courage to

cross the bridge (evolve) not knowing what is ahead. My intuition was being strengthened as I accepted a symbol of change (coin).

Fourth Chakra: Did I have to pay a cost for ascending from one level to another? My self-esteem, confidence, honor, and personal boundaries were strong, but to evolve further, I had to have a different power (coin). The coin of the evolved perspective was given to me as a grace by one who gives all grace.

Fifth Chakra: When the Hopi Indians say, "Keep the top of your head open," it is their way of saying our "Have a nice day." In their sensitive world view, this is an injunction to keep oneself consciously connected to a higher form of spiritually inspired intuition (Swan in Doore, 1988, p. 158).

As I accepted the new energy (power) my thought was, "I have the faith that I am led in the right direction by the Divine. What do I need now for this part of the journey?"

Continuing to work with the energy centers will help me to be sensitive to where my energy is blocked; working with my archetypes will show me the issues that need to be examined before I can move on. These are the power tools at my disposal.

June 1, 1995

I am stepping off my bridge. There are several steps down off the bridge. I look around and there are several people waiting there.

Many of us need to cross many bridges to continue to grow toward our completion, or our *becoming*. Some counselors suggest that clients who need to cross a bridge should physically walk across a bridge as a ritual, being conscious of what is happening spiritually and psychologically by making the ritual concrete and thereby reinforcing the inner process.

We are called to be "living bridges" in our lives, by using our hearts, minds, spirits, faith, prayers, dreams, intuition, love, (our power) as bridges to bring about positive changes in our lives, our communities, our organizations, our culture, and our world.

Summary of Waking Dream 38

Archetype: My Bridge acting on the Spiritual level and aligning with:

Sixth Chakra: I had made a conscious choice to step down from My Bridge into a new land (new reality) that is different; however, I was not alone. There were those who waited for me. Did they make the trip before me? Was this an ordination, a call to service for others? They seemed to be waiting *for me.*

It is interesting to note that I began two more groups this year (in my outer life). They are for HIV-AIDS infected women and for women with dissociative disorders.

July 1, 1995

All of "my people," Shaman, Wise Ones, People of Light, Angels, My Little Girl, Black Madonna, are on my bridge with me. We have come back about one-fourth of the way across for a purpose. As we all stand together, we are absorbed into each other. We become a strong, strong Light Person (at least I think that's how we look). We are all one.

Jung believed that if one's psyche could be viewed as a bridge between the transcendent power (the transcendent function inherent in the collective unconscious) and one's physical body, healing, that is, healing from a religious source, could be experienced. Kelsey (1981) points out that the archetypes are a kind of bridge themselves, linking the conscious with the collective unconscious, the individual present with the collective past.

Summary of Waking Dream 39

Archetypes: All previous ones, My Bridge acting on the Spiritual level and aligning with:

Fourth Chakra: The symbolic meaning of this chakra's Christian Sacrament of Marriage is that one must be in union with one's own personality and spirit first before creating an intimate other partnership.

Seventh Chakra: All of the archetypes appeared to me. They were my allies, teachers, guides, healers and friends. They were to always serve my best interests. We stepped back onto My Bridge for a ritual. I experienced their strength and their gifts in a new way as I lived my purpose (continued on my journey). We knew each other well and we honored each other. This mystic connection was to serve as a means to further my *becoming*. Each archetype will evolve and each energy center will evolve in a spiritual alchemical process.

As we stood together we became one; the giftedness and strengths of each was now integrated into the one, a synergy that made the one stronger than the sum of each. We were ready to live the ongoing mystery toward integration and transformation.

Eighth Chakra: The eighth chakra is located in the area of archetypal agreements which were made before birth. This agreement or sacred contract is a growth contract. The archetypes are available to help us live out the sacred contract, those divine lessons that we agree to learn in Earth School (Myss, 1995, lecture). By aligning the archetype with the energy centers, a more or less consistent flow of power is available for the completion of that sacred contract.

July 15, 1995

I am aware that I am on an entirely new Path. It is red brick, rather wide, and is built up on each side so that one may stop and rest.

Summary of Waking Dream 40

Archetype: New Path acting on the Spiritual level and aligning with all chakras:

I was now on a new Path (new perspective) or rather a continuation of My Path, but from a different perspective. I was on red brick, not dirt; this Path was wider, more defined. It was comforting that I was still grounded in the positive tribal (red). Clear space on either side invited one to sit and rest, meeting many others who also journey.

The atmosphere was different, lighter, brighter. It was easier to breathe; the air was cleaner. It felt like prayer here. Although I was alone, I felt at one with everything. I felt stronger, clearer, more purposeful. I have endured and now I will thrive as I continually align my will to Divine Will. I am confident that all of my images and dreams past, present, and future come in the service of my health and wholeness, and that even though I do not understand all of them, they will continue to do their dynamic work in my best interest.

I was eager to continue my journey. With each step I was becoming who I already am. That was enough.

November 8, 1995

I am on my path, but it goes around in a circle. I find myself inside the circle. People come and go, in and out of the circle, but I stay.

"You paint with light."

"You see music."

"You hear beauty."

Something has been completed.

Campbell (1994) defined synesthesia as the ability to hear colors and to see sounds. This noted expert on the mysteries of color and sound believes that synesthesia may be one of the most important healing modalities we have, in which the association of one sense is enhanced by another sense, yet the experience will be individual and unique. In ancient Greece, the ability of "feeling together" was essential to the healing arts.

Somé (1994) reports that in Dagara tradition one *hears* smell, one does not smell something. That which is picked up by the olfactory sense is sound being heard in that way. The same applies to the tactile sense. But you can both hear and see taste.

Bruyere (1994) writes that some energy healers are able to "hear" the sound of color being channeled into the body. In addition to "feeling" and "hearing" color, clairvoyants are able to see energies and auric fields.

Summary of Waking Dream 41

Archetype: Wisdom acting on the Spiritual Level and aligning with:

Sixth Chakra: This message seemed to be about irrational possibilities; of coloring outside the lines; of breaking out of restricting boxes; of illusory limitation. I was reminded that much of the spiritual journey consists of dismantling the rational mind.

People went in and out of the circle (a symbol of completion; unity) and I stayed. Did this say something about my path of service? Was this message one of ordination or initiation? Was the calling a result of being able to see or to know in a different way, with a different perspective or an irrational view? Or was this about symbolic sight, the ability to see through illusion and grasp the energy (power) or Divine reasoning behind the scenes?

Sixth chakra energies say, "Let go of how you think things should be. You *may* be able to paint with light, see music, and hear beauty. Thinking that you cannot do these 'irrational' things may be the only reason you cannot. Wake up to outrageous possibilities that invite miracles."

I have the distinct knowing, a spiritual intuition, that something has been completed. This image resonated in my soul and I knew that some soul work had been accomplished. Physical and psychological work had also been accomplished, as evidenced by less physical pain, fewer symptoms and a happier, more productive life lived closer to the Divine. Truly, I have been gifted by God's healing grace through the power of the images.

CHAPTER 4

RESULTS

I believe that I have shown in this study a progression of healing on the physical, psychological and spiritual levels and that there have been alignments and integrations of archetypes and chakras; therefore, the answer to my research question is yes. It has been possible to track the interaction of archetypal images on my body's chakra system. This process was accessed through the practice of Biogenics and this synergism produced the holistic healing that I have experienced. In this chapter, I detail the results of this process. This chapter is divided into three sections: each section detailing and interpreting a specific type of results.

Section one demonstrates, in table form, the results of the levels of activity (maturity) of archetypes in response to 41 specific dream images and the levels of chakra activity in response to 41 specific dream images.

Section two consists of the comparison of two clinical Symptom Indexes. The first index was completed as a part of the initial assessment procedures when I entered the Shealy Pain and Rehabilitation Clinic in 1988. The other index was completed when I attended a workshop led by Dr. Norm Shealy in 1999. Both were compiled by Dr. Shealy. One was copyrighted in 1988, the other was a revision dated 1999. They are essentially the same instrument, but the 1999 index was revised to eliminate non-essential wording.

Section three consists of a summary of original poetry that was written over an 18 month period about mid-way through the preparation of this dissertation. These poems were pivotal to the continuation and final preparation of this study.

RESULTS SECTION ONE

Even though I limited the number of dream images in this study (41 out of about 500) there is, I believe, evidence of the spiraling evolutionary movement over the seven-year study period. (See tables 1, 2, 3 and 4.) As the tables show, the results are heavily weighted toward the physical or tribal in the early years. The chakra response is weighted toward movement in the lower chakras. This was also the time when I was healing the fastest. I was being flooded with healing imagery as though this process had been *just waiting* to happen, impatient to do its work. During this time, I was experiencing less pain in the knees, hips, and lower back. I had no flare-ups from the Epstein-Barr virus, and few problems with allergies. I could feel that I was becoming more whole psychologically, physically, and spiritually. I now believe that this healing was the result, to a great extent, of the archetypal and chakra response to dream images during Biogenics. This process continued through the years, reflecting an upward progression from tribal (physical) through psychological (personal) and through the lower and middle chakras. (See tables 1, 2, 3 and 4.)

In 1992, a change occurs where the dream images shift into a decidedly spiritual emphasis. Spiritual archetypes (angels and other spiritual beings, Wisdom as Holy Spirit) aligned with the upper chakras, although all of the chakras were sometimes affected. I was becoming more prayerful, thoughtful, and intuitive as the upper chakras were being empowered. I had much less worry and depression and a much clearer sense of personal mission and community service.

I believe that these tables show that there is a strong connection between archetypes and chakras in my dream images. In other words, I believe they show a direct link between the three levels of personal power and responsibility (physical, psychological, spiritual) and the eight levels of energy and empowerment (chakras).

Table 1
Archetypal Level of Activity (Maturity)
in Response to Dream Image

DREAM IMAGE

	1	2	3	4	5	6	7	8	9	10	11	12	13	14	15	16	17	18	19	20	21
Spiritual (Symbolic)				★		★		★				★		★	★			★		★	
Psychological (Personal)		★			★	★			★	★	★		★		★	★				★	
Physical (Tribal)	★	★	★	★	★	★	★		★	★	★		★			★	★		★	★	★

DREAM IMAGE

	22	23	24	25	26	27	28	29	30	31	32	33	34	35	36	37	38	39	40	41	
Spiritual (Symbolic)	★		★	★		★	★	★	★	★	★	★	★	★	★	★	★	★	★	★	
Psychological (Personal)		★	★	★	★	★															
Physical (Tribal)		★		★	★	★							★	★							

★Indicates Single Dream Image

Table 2
Number of Dream Image Responses
on Each Archetypal Level

Level	Frequency	Percentage
Spiritual	26	63
Psychological	15	37
Physical	22	51

Table 3
Level of Chakra Activity in Response to Dream Image

DREAM IMAGE

CHAKRA	1	2	3	4	5	6	7	8	9	10	11	12	13	14	15	16	17	18	19	20	21
8														★							
7														★	★			★		★	
6					★	★					★			★	★			★		★	
5				★						★				★				★		★	
4						★			★	★		★	★			★				★	
3	★	★	★		★		★	★	★			★			★	★				★	★
2	★	★			★		★	★		★	★					★				★	
1	★	★	★	★	★	★	★	★	★	★	★	★	★		★	★	★	★	★	★	★

DREAM IMAGE

CHAKRA	22	23	24	25	26	27	28	29	30	31	32	33	34	35	36	37	38	39	40	41	
8																		★	★		
7	★			★			★	★	★	★	★	★	★					★	★		
6	★		★	★		★		★			★	★			★		★		★	★	
5	★	★	★		★	★	★	★							★	★			★		
4	★				★		★	★		★	★		★			★		★	★		
3	★	★						★								★			★		
2	★	★						★						★					★		
1	★	★			★	★		★		★	★		★	★					★		

★Indicates Single Dream Image

Table 4
Number of Dream Image Responses
on Each Chakra Level

Chakra Number	Frequency	Percentage
8	3	7
7	15	37
6	18	44
5	15	37
4	17	41
3	17	41
2	14	34
1	29	71

RESULTS SECTION TWO

Table 5
Comparison of Symptom Indexes Results

Year	Factor	Percentage
1988	Symptom Index (43 items out of possible 162)	27
1999	Symptom Index (12 items out of possible 165)	7

The result was most impressive considering the 11 year span of time between the completion of the indexes. One might expect more, not fewer symptoms related to the aging process. An analysis of these two instruments indicates that healing (as evidenced by fewer symptoms) occurred on all levels. Symptoms that remain are chiefly in the lower chakras where much of the physical dis-ease was located and where the most healing was needed in 1988. Soon after I completed the 1999 index, my doctor discovered that my ears contained a considerable built-up of hardened wax, which is directly related to two of the checked items on the 1999 index; thus, an additional two symptoms were eliminated. Again, I believe that these largely clinical results support my basic research question in an objective, measurable way.

RESULTS SECTION THREE

This section includes just five poems selected from my collection of twenty original poems which supports and answers the basic research question in a unique, surprising and creative way. The answer is affirmative and it happened in the following way (which itself is a result).

I was stuck about half way through this dissertation. I had too much material; it was too subjective; I had no focus. Everything was a muddle. I couldn't sleep, my neck hurt; my shoulders ached; my hand hurt from so much writing. I considered giving up. At that point, I had an idea (intuition). What if I just tried to capture the qualities of the archetypes as I saw them in my images? I put pen to paper — but instead of writing whole sentences, I began to create poetic imagery. I was mystified! I had never written poetry; never particularly wanted to do so.

Then, the light came on and I understood that I had been gifted with a classic example of another, unique way archetypes work. The poet archetype had been activated by heightened intuition which came about in response to a crisis. Poetic imagery became the link between or the level between the archetypal image and rational expression; it clarified and supported that three-level process so that I could find a focus and an understanding from a different perspective. This shift of consciousness broke my inertia. As the poetry flowed, I felt much better physically, psychologically and spiritually.

The maturity of the archetypes became evident in the tone, quality, and messages of the poetry. First, the poems are about tribal perceptions and concerns and feature the little girl or child archetype and the Wise Ones on the tribal level. My Journey and My Path archetypes as expressed in poetic imagery carried the messages of safety, stability, gratitude, and self-esteem. These mirror the lower chakra energies. As the archetypes mature, the process of individuation and psychological maturation are reflected in the poems. Issues of meaning and purpose, of becoming conscious of who I already am, the reframing of the meaning of wellness and healing are emphasized. I felt increasingly confident, hopeful, and thankful. My body responded by being healthier, more resilient.

Spiritually mature archetypes are reflected in the later poems. The higher energies of angels, People of Light, and Wisdom at the Holy Spirit level are found here. Spiritual alchemy, eternal paradox, soul wisdom, the levels of prayer, and the certainty about who and whose I am are spiritual themes in these poems. The last few poems describe the archetype of my New Path, (new consciousness) as I cross My Bridge (big transition). These poems echo the need for a new spiritual perspective that can encompass my new way of being, a perspective that elevates healing and wholeness to an enlightened lifestyle and asks the question expressed in the poem on the following page.

Can I be holy (whole enough)

That my life song blends with the hymn

Bursting from God's heart

Singing Wisdom

Into

Knowing?

Grace

My little girl waits to love me back to myself

All of my strivings to understand The

Journey

All of my efforts to discern The Will

dim

As I receive her energy of promise

As I absorb her innocent wisdom

I can _be_ anywhere

I can _be_ everywhere

When I open to God's specific energy called

grace

Paradox

Wise Ones believe that life is a sacred journey
of paradox and contradiction.

Forward may not bring progress
Pausing may be moving ahead
Turning inward may nudge us upward

Wise Ones know

Paths may _be_ purpose
Journeys may _be_ destination

Labyrinth

Illness can be a God centered labyrinth
Strong seeking hearts understand
its intent
its design
its language
its gifts

Within its cloistered center
Illness becomes Wellness

As we are led along its spiral path
We heal
from
the
inside
out.

The Search

We yearn to find our place
We are

      seekers who need more than shelter
      pilgrims who need more than warmth

We search for

      the wellspring of the soul
      the vision of the spirit
      the lodestone of the self

We worry how distant our journey
      Unaware we have already arrived
      Complete
        Safe
      In Holy Arms

Wisdom

How, then, shall we live?
Passionately enough that we risk being
tossed into the quicksand of injustice
and yet speak
shaken to our depths by another's agony
and yet abide
lifted out of complacency and hurled at deceit
and yet stand

Can we live whole enough
that ego does not dictate
action, reaction, inaction

Can we live aware enough
that we see more harm in caring too little
than in caring too much

Can we live real enough
that we trust our hearts to lead us
to treasure and purpose

Can we live humble enough
that pride does not require decisions
determined by loss or gain

Can we live holy enough
that our life song blends with the hymn
bursting from God's heart
Singing Wisdom
into
Knowing.

CHAPTER 5

RESEARCH IMPLICATIONS
AND DISCUSSION

I believe that this study shows that a system of deep relaxation and neuromuscular re-education can be the catalyst for the activation of archetypes from the collective unconscious. They can align with the energy system of the body to produce a progression of healing on many levels. While relief from chronic pain syndrome was the original intent, my holistic healing therapy went far beyond and above this purpose. In my case, it actually became an integral component of the process of individuation.

Can this study be replicated? Further studies are indicated for several very practical reasons: This therapy is very cost effective; there are few, if any, chemical medications involved; there are few visits to doctors' offices, no insurance claims, and the patient assumes control and responsibility for the time and conditions of the therapy. Beyond these benefits, there are indications that deep, multi-level healing of body, mind and spirit can occur with regular, intentional application of this therapy.

As I researched and prepared this dissertation, I became aware of avenues of inquiry that would be natural extensions of the study but were beyond the parameters of my topic. While there are many possibilities, there are, I believe, six implications that present interesting opportunities for research.

Some of these implications involve archetypes and chakras, while others are drawn from other key concepts of the study. A discussion of each implication follows.

Implication 1

One of the most interesting aspects of my study was gaining the understanding of some of the many ways archetypes work: their purpose, intent, and function. I was intrigued, especially, by the way archetypes appear in response to needs which are largely unconscious, in many cases in response to trauma or crisis.

In my work with women survivors of severe abuse who have been diagnosed with Dissociative Identity Disorder (DID) or Multiple Personality Disorder (MPD), I have become aware of how archetype-like multiple personalities appear to be. There are often wounded children, protectors, prostitutes, care givers, and teachers in the constellations of personalities. In addition, there are often artists and warriors.

Although I am not the primary therapist for these women, I spend two hours with them each week and they become quite open. I suggested that we study an overview of archetypes. They were very interested as they recognized many similarities between their different personalities and the archetypes. It gave them a new positive way to look at themselves.

Relatively little is known about DID which is, I believe, much more common than acknowledged by mental health professionals. A study which explores dissociative personalities as archetypes in form, intent, and function would be enlightening. It could possibly bring a needed breakthrough in perspective on DID that encourages more accurate, effective, compassionate treatment by the mental health community and the larger community toward those with this disorder. I have come to realize that there are few special populations as under-served as this one.

Implication 2

An implication that is particularly interesting to me is further study of prayer combined with spontaneous imagery in a healing (wholeness) process. I began to see my relaxation time as sacred time; as I reflected that insight to a friend, she indicated that my whole seven-year experience seemed to be all about prayer. I have an intuition that she is right; however, I have found that my concept of prayer has changed tremendously. Just as there have been spiraling progressions of healing on other levels, my understanding of prayer has undergone the same progression.

As I began each pain management period, I said a simple, brief prayer asking for protection and healing according to God's will for my life. After a year or so, I noticed that something was different. It felt as though I was being prayed and, although I still began each session with prayer, I knew that I was being graced with more than I asked, or perhaps I had not realized just for what I had prayed.

After some months, I found that there was another change. Although it is difficult to put into words, I felt that I *was* prayer and words meant very little. Again, after several months at this place in my sacred journey, I sensed another change. I was experiencing a unity with all that was new. It was my understanding that I was made prayer for others. It was at this point that I began to see more clearly that God's will for me *is* to become who I *already* am and that prayer is the divine magnetic energy that keeps me focused and growing toward that goal. It is my belief that imagery has supported this process at every stage of the journey.

Adding the richness of imagery to the mystery of prayer as a means of achieving wholeness (holiness) is an experience similar to those described in classical mysticism. I am sure that there are other future revelations but at this time, I can see this connection clearly enough to title my dissertation *The Power of Image, The Gift of Grace*. I now view my illness as an essential step on my way to wholeness or individuation or salvation, keeping me on the path until I have found, or the healing has found me, that not only relieved much of the physical pain but has changed my whole perspective of pain, prayer, purpose and power.

Can the process of this experience be distilled and replicated? I am intrigued by the possibility.

Implication 3

Through the completion of this study, I now believe that archetypal healing could become a significant partner with many other healing modalities. An understanding of archetypal process, intent and purpose linked with existing psychological, physical and spiritual developmental models could bring clarity, focus and an understanding of holistic healing on many levels.

Further, linking the study of archetypes with other areas of learning such as theology, science, psychology, and history would create a conceptual synergy that would benefit our understanding of and appreciation for our complex world and our relationship to every thing in it. It would help us to discover who we are and where we come from, and help us to acknowledge our responsibilities for ourselves and others. The conscious integration of these innate patterns of behavior into our everyday lives would bring clarity and a focus that would enrich us every day.

For example, Strauss and Howe (1997) are two scholars and historians who recognize the notable effects of intentional archetypal involvement in broad historical terms. In their book, *The Fourth Turning*, they link each of our present generations with a recurring sequence of four generational archetypes that have appeared throughout history. Thus, they have created an American prophecy which predicts both great crisis and great opportunity. Their use of historical, generational patterns help to clarify the understanding of our collective past and predictions of our future. The study of archetypal influences in other fields of inquiry might be helpful, timely, and refreshing.

Implication 4

As I experienced the body releases that came with archetype and chakra alignment, I began to relate this concept to my clinical work, and I began to see another possible avenue of research.

It is well documented that persons who have been traumatized, especially in early childhood, store memories in body tissue. The energy system is contaminated by these traumas, causing the chakras to lose their ability to transmit energy. Achterberg (1985) calls this disorder alexithymia meaning "without words for feelings" (p. 123). Working with a body energy therapist often releases these memories that can release the blocked energy flow. Possible research would pair a psychological therapist and an energy therapist in joint sessions with the client. As body memories are released, the psychological, cognitive and spiritual aspects of the memories can be processed. This synergistic healing process would be multi-layered and holistic. I have worked briefly in this therapeutic process and the client often speaks of how much better she feels, how much deep, hard work has been accomplished in a short time, and how gentle the process. This therapy should be researched and studied as a companion to other therapies.

Implication 5

As a result of some of my waking dreams, especially the ones involving cleansing my generational line, together with my reading about Christian generational healing and my work with women survivors, I have been made aware that there are ancient connections that are not DNA exclusive. Generational legacies often carry patterns of generational abuses (incest, suicide, addictions, cult involvement, alcoholism) that keep perpetuating dis-ease, generation after generation.

After considerable research, I found that there is a recently recovered "Healing the Family Tree" Christian ministry that is experiencing success (MacNutt 2000). This is a powerful spiritual healing technique, actually a form of intercessory prayer, that has great potential for healing through intentional forgiveness, reconciliation and restoration. This is also an area of the healing ministry that can deal with issues of spiritual oppression that few therapists or clergy are aware of or are trained to treat. Survivors have taught me that if true healing is to be accomplished, liberation from the brokenness and negative patterns of ancestors is essential, and we have begun to use this kind of spiritual healing in our groups on a limited scale.

A study of the process and effects of generational healing for all whose ancient connections carry dis-ease, which includes survivors of abuse, might offer another healing modality for therapists and healing for a sizable segment of the population whose dis-ease is invisible to most and ignored by many.

Implication 6

As I experienced the healing that occurred during Biogenics exercises, it seemed to me that a modification of this safe, economical, drug-free method of pain and stress management has great potential for preventing and/or healing all kinds of dis-ease. Further, it would be an efficient way of accessing the unconscious, that deep reservoir of images, myth, and dreams which carry evolutionary energies that correct, compensate, enrich, and teach.

Pelletier (1977) explains that two methods, autogenics and visualization, are potentially powerful, not necessarily because they would correct pathology but because they may be powerful techniques in a holistic approach to the *prevention* of disease. By using these self-regulatory techniques, subtle dysfunctions may be recognized and corrected before health is compromised. Children in several European countries are taught these effective techniques in elementary school with the result that they learn to manage stress at an early age.

A variety of similar straight forward, effective techniques could be introduced in our schools, hospitals, churches, health centers, and work places, teaching a good portion of the population to experience and maintain harmony of body, mind and spirit. This approach would almost surely cut health costs, reduce violence and competition and release creativity.

What a concept; relaxation, not Ritalin! Visualization, not violence!

As I conclude this study, this part of my journey, I believe that I have answered my stated research question. I am now aware of a much deeper, more profound question. It is best expressed by the last line of my concluding poem.

Can I be
Individual
Indivisible
Honest to God?

I will be growing into the answer to this question
for the rest of my life.

Honest

I can no longer live an around-the-edge kind of life
of second-hand beliefs
handed-down codes
broken-in conduct

Dare I say that I want
the mess of a well-lived untidy life
the chaos that comes with spontaneous openness
the vulnerability of a wide-open heart
the faith that demands unconditional love

Dare I ask God to
strip away my illusion of security
tear away my treasured stuff
heal my addiction to conformity
invite me to confront my worth

Perhaps.

Could I, then
express my deep body-wisdom
feel my thinking
know the knowing beyond safe thought
plumb the deep mysteries of the spirit
trust my practical intuition

Could I Be
Individual
Indivisible
Honest to God?

BIBLIOGRAPHY

Absher, T. (1990). *Men and the Goddess: Feminine Archetypes in Western Literature*. Rochester, VT: Park Street Press.

Achterberg, J. (1985). *Imagery in Healing: Shamanism and Modern Medicine*. Boston: Shambhala.

Adler, M. J. (1982). *The Angels and Us*. New York: Collier Books.

Amerson, R. (1999). *The Power of Love*. [On-Line]. Hostname: www.anew-worldrising.com/takeaction.

Andrews, T. (1997). *Animal-Speak: The Spiritual and Magical Powers of Creatures Great and Small*. St. Paul, MN: Llewellyn.

Arrien, A. (1993). *The Four-fold Way: Walking the Paths of the Warrior, Teacher, Healer, and Visionary*. San Francisco: HarperSanFrancisco.

Atwater, D. (1965). *The Penguin Dictionary of Saints*. Baltimore: Penguin.

Bancroft, A. (1989). *Weavers of Wisdom: Women Mystics of the Twentieth Century*. New York: Arkana.

Becker, R. O. & Selden, G. (1985). *The Body Electric: Electromagnetism and the Foundation of Life*. New York: William Morrow and Company.

Benson, H. (1975). *The Relaxation Response.* New York: Morrow.

Benson, R. (1998). *Living Prayer*. New York: Jeremy P. Tarcher/Putnam.

Black E. (1953). *The Sacred Pipe*. (Recorded and Edited by J. S. Brown.) Norman, OK: University of Oklahoma Press.

Blavatsky, H.P. (03/14/2000). *The Number Seven* [On-Line]. Hostname: www.blavatsby.net Directory: blavatsky/arts/number seven.num

Bly, R. and Woodman, M. (1998). *The Maiden King: The Reunion of Masculine and Feminine*. New York: Henry Holt.

Bolen, J. S. (Speaker). (1991). *Wise Woman Archetype: Menopause as Initiation.* (Cassette Recording Tape No. A137). Boulder, CO: Sounds True Audio.

Borg, M. (1995). *Meeting Jesus Again for the First Time*. San Francisco: Harper Collins.

Borg, M. (1998). *The God We Never Knew*. San Francisco: Harper Collins.

Borysenko, J. (1988). *Guilt is the Teacher, Love is the Lesson*. New York: Warner Books.

Borysenko, J. (1997). *The Way of the Mystic: Seven Paths to God*. Carlsbad, CA: Hay House.

Boyd, D. (1974). *Rolling Thunder*. New York: Random House.

Braden, G. (1997). *Walking Between the Worlds: The Science of Compassion*. Bellevue, WA: Radio Bookstore Press.

Braden, G. (1999). *Awakening to Zero Point: The Collective Initiation*. Bellevue, WA: Radio Bookstore Press.

Braud, W. and Anderson, R. (1998). *Transpersonal Research Methods for the Social Sciences: Honoring Human Experience.* Thousand Oaks, CA: Sage.

Brofman, M. (1998). Title of Article *The Chakras for Healing and Self-knowledge: A Visual Representation of the Body Mirror System*. [On-Line]. Avaliable: http//www.healer,ch/bmsarticle.htm.

Brown, J. E. (1982). *The Spiritual Legacy of the American Indian*. New York: Crossroad.

Bruyere, R. L. (1989). *Wheels of Light: Chakras, Auras, and the Healing Energy of the Body*. New York: Simon & Schuster.

Bruyere, R. L. (1991). *Wheels of Light: Chakras, Auras, and the Healing Energy of the Body*. New York: Simon & Schuster.

Bruyere, R. L. (1994). *Wheels of Light: Chakras, Auras, and the Healing Energy of the Body*. New York: Simon & Schuster.

Campbell, D. G. (1994, Autumn). *Colors and Sounds. Quest*, Vol.7, No. 3, 80 - 81.

Campbell, J. (1959). *The Masks of God: Primitive Mythology*. New York: Viking.

Campbell, J. (Ed.) (1970). *Myths, Dreams, and Religion*. Dallas, TX: Spring Publications.

Campbell, J. (1986). *The Inner Reaches of Outer Space: Metaphor as Myth and as Religion*. New York: Viking.

Carlson, R. and Shield, B. (Ed.) (1989). *Healers on Healing*. Los Angeles. Jeremy Tarcher, Inc.

Chopra, D. (1993). *Ageless Body, Timeless Mind*. New York: Harmony.

Cirlot, J. E. (1971, 2nd. Ad.) *A Dictionary of Symbols*. New York: Philosophical Library, Inc.

Clift, W. B. (1982). *Jung and Christianity: The Challenge of Reconciliation*. New York: Crossroad.

Clift, J. D. and Clift, W. B. (1992). *Symbols of Transformation in Dreams*. New York: Crossroad.

Coelho, P. (1998). *The Alchemist*. (1998). New York: Harper Collins.

DeQuincey, C. (May-June 2000). Consciousness: Truth or Wisdom? *IONS Noetic Sciences Review*. 8.

Doore, G. (1988). *Shaman's Path: Healing, Personal Growth, and Empowerment*. Boston: Shambhala.

Dossey, L. (1993). *Healing Words: The Power of Prayer and the Practice of Medicine*. New York: Harper Collins.

Dossey, L. (1996). *Prayer is Good Medicine: How to Reap the Healing Benefits of Prayer*. San Francisco: HarperSanFrancisco.

Edinger, E. F. (1992). *Ego and Archetype*. Boston: Shambhala.

Eisler, R. (1987). *The Chalice and the Blade: Our History, our Future*. Cambridge, MA: Harper & Row.

Eliade, M. (1991). *Images and Symbols: Studies in Religious Symbolism*. Princeton, NJ: Princeton University Press.

Emmons, M. L. (1978). *The Inner Source: A Guide to Meditative Therapy*. San Luis Obispo, CA. Impact Publishers.

Faraday, A. (1974). *The Dream Game*. New York: Harper.

Festival of Archetypal Psychology at Notre Dame. (Annual Conference). *Archetypal Psychology: Noted Scholars Examine the World of Archetypal Psychology*. (Cassette Recording Tape No. F004). Boulder, CO: Sounds True Recordings.

Feuerstein, G. (1991). *Sacred Paths: Essays on Wisdom, Love, and Mystical Realization*. Burdette, NY: Larson.

Fontana, D. (1993). *The Secret Language of Symbols*. San Francisco: Chronicle Books.

Fontana, D. (1994). *The Secret Language of Dreams*. San Francisco: Chronicle Books.

Foster, R. J. (1992). *Prayer: Finding the Heart's True Home*. San Francisco: HarperSanFrancisco.

Fox, M. (1979). *A Spirituality named Compassion*. San Francisco: Harper and Row.

Fox, M. (1983). *Original Blessings*. Santa Fe NM: Bear and Company.

Fox, M. (1988). *The Coming of the Cosmic Christ*. New York, Harper and Row.

Galde, P. (1988). *Crystal Healing: The Next Step*. St. Paul, MN: Llewellyn.

Gerber, R. (2000). *Vibrational Medicine for the 21st Century*. New York: Harper Collins.

Gibran, K. (1971). *The Prophet*. New York: Alfred A. Knopf.

Goldsmith, J. S. (1959). *The Art of Spiritual Healing*. New York: Harper.

Graham, B. (1975). *Angels, Angels: God's Secret Agents*. Dallas: Word Publishing.

Grassi, J. (1987). *Healing the Heart*. New York: Paulist Press.

Growther, J. (Ed.) et al. (1995). *Oxford Advanced Learner's Dictionary*. Oxford: University Press.

Harner, M. (1982). *The Way of the Shaman: A Guide to Power & Healing*. San Francisco: Harper & Row.

Heaney, J. (1984). *The Sacred and the Psychic: Parapsychology and Christian Theology*. New Jersey: Paulist Press.

Henry, J. P. (1992). *Instinct, Archetypes, and Symbols: An Approach to the Physiology of Religious Experience*. (Edited by W. P. Frost.) Dayton, OH: College Press.

Heron, B. (1989). *Channels of Healing Prayer*. Notre Dame, IN: Ave Maria Press.

Hoeller, S. A. (1989). *Jung and the Lost Gospels: Insights into the Dead Sea Scrolls and the Nag Hammadi Library*. Wheaton, IL: Quest Books.

Houston, J. (1997). *A Passion for the Possible: A Guide to Realizing your True Potential*. San Francisco: HarperSanFrancisco.

Howard, J. M. (1992). *Commune with the Angels: A Heavenly Handbook*. Virginia Beach, VA: A.R.E. Press.

Hunter, H. (1997 March/April). The Mystical Power of Poetry. *Intuition 15*, 33.

International Society for the Study of Subtle Energies and Energy Medicine — ISSSEEM. (Annual Conference of ISSSEEM). (1998). *Energy Medicine: Subtle Energies, Consciousness, and the New Science of Healing*. (Cassette Recording No. F067). Boulder, CO: Sounds True Audio.

Jamal, M. (1987). *Shape Shifters: Shaman Women in Contemporary Society*. New York: Arkana.

Jones, A. (1985). *Soul Making: The Desert Way of Spirituality*. San Francisco: Harper & Row.

Jones, A. (1992). *Journey into Christ*. Philadelphia, PA: Trinity Press and Boston, MA: Cowley Publications.

Jung, C. G. (1933). *Modern Man in Search of a Soul*. New York: A Harvest Book, Harcourt and Brace.

Jung, C. G. (1958). *Psyche and Symbol: A Selection from Writings of C. G. Jung*. (V. S. de Laszlo, Ed.) New York: Anchor.

Jung, C. G., von Franz, M. L., Henderson & L., Jaffe, A. (1964). *Man and his Symbols*. New York: Dell Publishing.

Kavanaugh, K., OCD & O. Rodreguiz, O., OCD, (Trans. 1979). *The Interior Castle*. New York: Paulist Press

Kelsey, M. T. (1974). *Myth, History and Faith*. New York: Paulist Press.

Kelsey, M.T. (1976). *The Other Side of Silence: A Guide to Christian Meditation*. New York: Paulist Press.

Kelsey, M.T. (1978). *Discernment: A Study in Ecstasy and Evil*. New York: Paulist Press.

Kelsey, M.T. (1982). *Christo-Psychology*. New York: Crossroad.

Kelsey, M.T. (1991). *God, Dreams and Revelation: A Christian Interpretation of Dreams — Revised and Expanded Edition*. Minneapolis, MN: Augsburg.

Kelsey, M.T. (1992). *Dreamquest: Native American Myth and the Recovery of the Soul*. Rockport, MA: Element.

Leeming, D. A. (1990). *The World of Myth*. New York: Oxford University Press.

Leichtman, R. and Joepekse, C. (1989). *Healing Lines: A New Interpretation of the I Ching for Healing Inquiries*. Columbus, OH: Ariel Press.

LeShan, L. (1974). *The Medium, the Mystic, and the Physicist: Toward a General Theory of the Paranormal*. New York: Viking.

Luke, H. M. (1975). *Dark Wood to White Rose: A Study of Meanings in Dante's Divine Comedy*. Pecos, NM: Dove.

Lukeman, A. (1990). *What Your Dreams can Teach You*. St. Paul, MN: Llewellyn.

Lüscher, M. (1969). *The Lüscher Color Test*. (Translated and edited by I. Scott.). New York: Simon & Schuster.

MacNutt, F. (Spring 2000). Being freed from generational bondage. *Christian Healing Ministries, Volume 13, Issue 1* 1.

Matthews, D. A. (with Clark, C.). (1998). *The Faith Factor: Proof of the Healing Power of Prayer*. New York: Viking.

May, G. (1988). *Addiction and Grace*. San Francisco: Harper & Row.

May, G. (1992). *Care of Mind, Care of Spirit: Psychiatric Dimensions of Spiritual Direction*. San Francisco: Harper & Row.

McAll, K. (1982). *Healing the Family Tree*. Great Britian: Biddles Ltd., Greilford and King's Lynn.

Moody, R. with Perry, P. (1991). *Coming Back: A Psychiatrist Explores Past-life Journeys*. New York: Bantam Books.

Moore, R. and Gillette, D. (1990). *King, Warrior, Magician, Lover: Rediscovering the Archetypes of the Mature Masculine*. San Francisco: HarperSan Francisco.

Moss, R. (1997). *Dream Gates*. (Cassette Recording No. F065). Boulder, CO: Sounds True Audio.

Mother Teresa. (1996). *Meditations from a Simple Faith*. New York: Ballentine.

Mulholland, M. R. (1985). *Shaped by the Word: The Power of Scripture in Spiritual Formation*. Nashville, TN: The Upper Room.

Myss, C. (1995). *Personal Pain and Stress Management Workbook*. Unpublished manuscipt, Part 1.

Myss, C. (1996). *Anatomy of the Spirit*. New York: Harmony Books.

Myss, C. (1998). *Spiritual Power, Spiritual Practice*. (Cassette Recording No. F389). Boulder, CO: Sounds True Audio.

Nottingham, T. (1993). *Written on Our Hearts: The Practice of Spiritual Transformation*. Greenwood, IN: Inner Life Publication.

Open Bible, The. (1979). *New American Standard Bible*. New York: Thomas Nelson Publisher.

Pagels, E. (1979). *The Gnostic Gospels*. New York: Random House.

Pascal, E. (1992). *Jung to Live By*. New York: Warner Books.

Pearson, C. S. (1986). *The Hero Within: Six Archetypes to Live by*. San Francisco: Harper & Row.

Pearson, C. S. (1991). *Awakening the Heroes Within: Twelve Archetypes to Help Us Find Ourselves and Transform Our World*. San Francisco: HarperCollins.

Peck, M. S. (1995). *In Search of Stones: A Pilgrimage of Faith, Reason, and Discovery*. New York: Hyperion.

Pelletier, K. (1977). *Mind as Healer, Mind as Slayer: A Holistic Approach to Preventing Stress Disorders*. New York: Delacorte.

Pherigo, L. P. (1992). *The Great Physician Luke: The Healing Stories*. Nashville, TN: Abingdon.

Rain, M.S. (1990). *Earthway: A Native American Visionary's Path to Total Mind, Body, and Spirit Health*. New York: Pocket Books.

Remen, R. N. (1996). *Kitchen Table Wisdom: Stories that Heal*. New York: Riverhead Books.

Robinson, L. (1976). *Edgar Cayce's Story of the Origin and Destiny of Man*. New York: Berkley.

Roche de Coppens, P. (1994, Autumn). Psychosynthesis and the Spiritual Traditon. *Quest* 50.

Roth, R. (Speaker). (1994). *Spiritual Healing: Merging Medicine and Meditation*. (Cassette Recording Live 11-12-1994). Indianapolis: Great Lakes Training Associates.

Sams, J. and Carson, D. (1988) *Medicine Cards: The Discovery of Power through the Ways of Animals*. Santa Fe, New Mexico: Bear and Company.

Sanford, J. A. (1987) *Dreams: God's Forgotten Language*. New York: Crossroad.

Sanford, J. A. (1987). *The Kingdom Within: The Inner Meaning of Jesus' Sayings*. San Francisco: Harper & Row.

Sanford, J. A. (1987). *The Man who Wrestled with God: Light from the Old Testament on the Psychology of Individuation*. New York: Paulist Press.

Sanford, J. A. (1992). *Healing Body & Soul: The Meaning of Illness in the New Testament and in Psychotherapy*. Louisville, KY: Westminster/John Knox Press.

Sanford, J. A. (1995). *Mystical Christianity: A Psychological Commentary on the Gospel of John*. New York: Crossroad.

Savary, L. (1984). *Dreams and Spiritual Growth: A Christian Approach to Dreamwork*. Ramsey, NJ: Paulist Press.

Schulz, M. L. (1998). *Awakening Intuition: Using your Mind-Body Network for Insight and Healing*. New York: Harmony Books.

Sharp, D. (1991). *C. G. Jung Lexicon: A Primer of Terms and Concepts*. Toronto: Inner City Books.

Shealy, C. N. (1986). *Biogenics Health Maintenance: Manual Self Health Systems*. Unpublished manuscript.

Shealy, C. N. (1995). *Personal Pain and Stress Management Workbook*. Unpublished manuscipt, Part 2.

Shealy, C. N. (1996). *Miracles Do Happen*. Rockport MA: Element Books.

Shealy, C. N. (1996). *The Self-Healing Workbook*. Rockport MA: Element Books.

Shealy, C. N. (1997). *Illustrated Encyclopedia of Healing Remedies*. Boston: Element Books.

Shealy, C. N. (1999). *Sacred Healing: The Curing Power of Energy and Spirituality*. Boston: Element Books.

Shealy, C. N. & Myss, C.M. (1993). *The Creation of Health*. Walpole MH: Stillpoint Publishing.

Siegel, B. (1977 Winter). Parabola: Myth, Tradition and the Search for Meaning. *A Way of Healing, xxii, 4.* 64.

Sinetar, M. (1992). *A Way without Words: A Guide for Spiritually Emerging Adults*. New York: Paulist Press.

Singer, J. (1994). *Boundaries of the Soul; the Practice of Jung's Psychology*. New York: Anchor Books, Division of Random House.

Somé, M. P. (1994). *Of Water and the Spirit: Ritual, Magic and Initiation in the Life of an African Shaman*. New York: Jeremy Tarcher/Putman Books.

Stapleton, M. (1982). *Concise Dictionary of Greek and Roman Mythology*. New York: Peter Bedrick Books.

Stapleton, M. (1986). *Concise Dictionary of Greek and Roman Mythology*. New York: Peter Bedrick Books.

Stein, M. (1998), *Jung's Map of the Soul: An Introduction*. Chicago: Open Court.

Stevens, J. & Stevens, L. (1988). *Secrets of Shamanism*. New York: Avon Books.

Storr, A. (1983). *The Essential Jung*. Princeton NJ: Princeton Press.

Strauss, W. & Howe, N. (1997). *The Fourth Turning: An American Prophecy*. New York: Broadway Books.

Taylor, J. (1992). *Where People Fly and Water Runs Uphill: Using Dreams to Tap the Wisdom of the Unconscious*. New York: Warner Books.

Underhill, E. (1961). *Mysticism*. New York: Dutton Books.

Ulanov, A. and Ulanov, B. (1982). *Primary Speech: A Psychology of Prayer*. Atlanta, GA: John Knox Press.

Vaughn, F. (1979). *Awakening Intuition*. New York: Doubleday Dell Publishing Group, Inc.

Villoldo, A. (2000). *Shaman, Healer, Sage: How to Heal Yourself and Others with the Energy Medicine of the Americas*. New York: Random House, Inc.

Walker, B. G. (1985). *The Crone: Women of Age, Wisdom and Power*. San Francisco: Harper & Row.

Walker, B. G. (1988). *The Woman's Dictionary of Symbols and Sacred Objects*. San Francisco: Harper & Row.

Walters, A. Lee. (1989). *The Spirit of Native America: Beauty and Mysticism in American Indian Art*. San Francisco: Chronicle.

Wauters, A. (1997). *Chakras and their Archetypes: Uniting Energy Awareness and Spiritual Growth*. Freedom, CA: Crossing Press.

Wiederkehr, M. (1988). *A Tree Full of Angels*. New York. Paulist Press.

Welch, J. (1982). *Spiritual Pilgrims: Carl Jung and Teresa of Avila*. New York: Paulist Press.

Whitmont, E. C. (1991). *The Symbolic Quest: Basic Concepts of Analytical Psychology*. Princeton, NJ: Princeton University Press.

Wolf, F. A. (1996). *The Spiritual Universe: How Quantum Physics Proves the Existence of the Soul*. New York: Simon & Schuster.

Woodman, M. (1996 October). Return of the Black Goddess. *Intuition, 14.*

Woodman, M. (Speaker). (1998). *Sitting by the Well: Bringing the Feminine to Consciousness through Language, Dreams, and Metaphors*. (Cassette Recording Tape No. F066). Boulder, CO: Sounds True Audio.

Woods, R. and Greenhouse, H. (1974). *The New World of Dreams: An Anthology*. New York: MacMillan.

Woodward, M. A. (1985). *Scars of the Soul: Holistic Healing in the Edgar Cayce Readings*. Columbus, OH: Brindabella Books.

Worrall, A. and Worrall, O. (1965). *The Gift of Healing: A Personal Story of Spiritual Therapy*. New York: Harper and Row.

Zachner, R. C. (1967). *Mysticism: Sacred and Profane*. New York: Oxford University.

Zukav, G. (1989). *The Seat of the Soul*. New York: Simon and Schuster.

INDEX